MW00679336

Angel

the true story of
an undeserved chance

PUBLISHED BY OWL OF HOPE
OUR WRITTEN LIVES OF HOPE, LLC
ALEXANDRIA, LOUISIANA
PRINTED IN THE U.S.A.

OWL of Hope provides publishing and technical assistance to authors in various educational, religious, and human service organizations. For information, visit www.owlofhope.com.

All Scripture quotations are from the Holy Bible, King James Version. Health Information is from government web sites in the public domain.

Any omission of credits is unintentional. Content is based on the memory of Angelena Cortello. Names have been changed, with the exception of Angelena "Angel" Cortello.

Library of Congress Cataloging-in-Publication Data
Hartman, Rachael, 1983—
Cortello, Angel, 1979—
        Angel: The True Story of an Undeserved Chance /
        Rachael Hartman / Angelena Cortello

Library of Congress Control Number: 2013909570
ISBN: 978-0-9894070-0-7 (paperback)
ISBN: 978-0-9894070-1-4 (electronic)

1. Addiction—Controversial literature. 2. Prostitution—Controversial literature. 3. Addiction Recovery—Interpretation. 4. Spiritual Life—Christianity. 5. Individual Biography.

Angel

the true story of
an undeserved chance

ANGELENA CORTELLO
AS TOLD TO RACHAEL HARTMAN

PUBLISHED BY
OUR WRITTEN LIVES OF HOPE

CONTENTS

PART 3—*Life Lessons*

Dedication

For all afflicted with addiction & mental illness
For all infected with HIV/AIDS
For all family members affected by these issues
ANGEL

For all who seek hope
For all who help others find hope
RACHAEL

A Note from Angel

There are two messages I want to send out to anyone who reads this book. The first is: if you have never gone down the self-destructive path I went down, you don't have to. The second is: if you have been down this path of darkness, you can change anytime you want to and live an abundant life with the consequences of your choices.

As well, I feel compelled to let people know that not everyone who is HIV positive caught the virus through making risky choices, the way I did. There are many innocent victims of the virus.

Not everyone will have the same experiences of recovery from addiction as I did. Not everyone will agree with everything in this book. This book holds my experiences, my life story, and I hope readers will be open to what I have to say.

Recovery has taught me to focus on similarities between others and myself instead of the differences between each of us. I hope something in this book will speak to your situation, give you a revelation, or maybe just a word of encouragement.

After starting work on this book in July of 2012, I began praying about what should be on the cover. My God spoke to my heart one word: dragonfly. When I started researching the meaning of the dragonfly, this is what I found.

The dragonfly represents:
- Gaining a new perspective through personal growth
- Seeing the deeper meaning of life
- Embracing the truth about self and rejecting lies
- Removing walls of perfection and allowing flaws

The dragonfly reminds me of my ongoing journey of transformation, change, deliverance, recovery, healing, and wholeness that is necessary for me to fulfill God's dream for my life. Thank you for taking the time to read this book.

If you need to contact me, please e-mail me at: **angelenacortello@bellsouth.net**

Acknowledgements

First and foremost, I want to thank my Lord and Savior, Jesus Christ, for everything He has done in my life. I also want to thank all of the wonderful people in my life who have helped me along the way. I love you all.

Frank & Cynthia Cortello
Amanda, Austin, Amelia & Isabelle
Karen & Steve Gissin
Angelina & Frank Cortello
Glenn & Lydia Cortello
Joann & David Peters

Anthony & Mickey Mangun	Marsha Abraham	Alexia Johnson
Terry & Melanie Shock	Jamie Albritton	Heather Knight
Robert & Terry Antoon	Abigail Aycock	Charlotte McCann
Jennifer & Steve Dean	Lane Aycock	Catherine Mills
Sandra & Greg Ellington	Anita Belgard	Tami Misse
Ruth & Armand Gissin	Rebecca Boyett	Adilya Murphy
Kevin & Pam Howard	Michelle Bryant	Patrick Nugent
Susan & Dwayne Scherer	Jennifer Danzy	Michael Paul
Paul & Karen Smith	Sarah Dowd	Devon Sanders
Darlene & David Vanduivendyk	Terri Eldridge	Linda Smith
Monica & Davis Wiggins	Naomi February	Annette Virok
Pauni Abbott	Bethany Fontenot	Ryan Wade
Mari Bobbitt	Debi Greene	Amber Wilkins
Nicole Brown	Heather Harper	Crystel Young
Pamela Nolde	Rachael Hartman	Tyler Young
Vani Marshall	Destiny Hawks	

A Note from Rachael

In June of 2001, I boarded an airplane in London, England, to return to Washington, D.C. after a youth mission trip to Kenya, Africa. I was seventeen and a recent high school graduate.

On the plane, I sat in my assigned seat next to a man I had never met before. He asked me where I was coming from and where I was going. I told the man about my desire to work in ministry. I had accepted my calling when I was ten years old and planned to go to Bible college.

The man seemed pleasantly surprised to hear of my plans. "So are you the kind of person that would help a prostitute find Jesus?" He asked me. With childlike faith, I answered "Yes."

I had no idea that at that very moment there was a girl named Angel, just a few years older than me, living on the streets in South Florida, prostituting to pay for her drug addiction. Eleven years later, I met Angel at a church service and we began to work on the book you now hold in your hands—a book that I hope helps many people find freedom in Christ.

Angel's story, as well as the stories of people she met on the streets, filled my heart with compassion and humility. I believe when we take the time listen to other's life stories, we are better able to understand outside perspectives and to make a positive difference in our world.

My life is totally different from Angel's, but I still understood her feelings and learned from her story. I hope that if you are like me and know nothing of street life, that you too can open your mind and heart and learn from Angel's story. I pray that as you read this book you will allow the light of compassion to warm your heart and spur you to reach out with understanding and grace to people. God bless you all.

Acknowledgements

I am eternally grateful to God for His grace, for filling me with His Spirit when I was eight years old, and for keeping me all of these years. I am thankful for the call to serve others that God has placed on my life, and for the creative energy He blessed me with.

I am especially thankful for my parents, Pastor and Chaplain, J.S. Hartman (LTC, U.S. Army, Retired) and Mrs. Patricia Hartman, for their faithfulness to God and each other throughout all seasons of their lives. I am thankful they shared their own personal life stories with me so that I have an understanding of all God saved our family from.

I am thankful for my sister, Tamara Hartman Munson and her husband Keith Munson, and the way they live grace and compassion. They consistently and selflessly help people in need.

I am thankful for my brother, Jeremy Hartman, his compassion and honesty, and for the positive way he approaches his own story of recovery.

Thank you to all of my friends for your support. To P.N., who edited the first draft. To Bethany Fontenot, who spent hours with me as we read through the manuscript, re-wrote and edited. To Sarah Dowd, who painted the dragonfly for the cover of the book.

Thank you to everyone who encouraged me. Your prayers and positive comments helped make me who I am today. Thank you to each minister, leader, teacher and professor who encouraged me and empowered me with the knowledge I needed to begin pursuing my God-given dreams.

SHATTERED

PART 1

I walked into the recovery meeting and sat in a chair next to my sponsor. Each person introduced themselves by name and addiction. "Hello. My name is Angel," I said to the recovery group. With a deep breath and these five words, I began to share my story. "I am an addict and I've been in recovery from crack addiction for ten years."

"Hello, Angel. Congratulations!" The recovery group responded in unison. There was a quiet murmur as several people commented on my achievement—ten years of freedom from addiction. That night's meeting leader stepped up and said, "Ten years! That is wonderful! We've been looking forward to meeting you and hearing your story of recovery!"

My sponsor stood and formally introduced me as the speaker for the night. She handed me a coin that represented ten years of recovery. "This is in recognition of your accomplishment," she said. "We're turning the floor over to you. Share your story with us!"

I gripped the coin as I moved to the podium to speak. "First, if you don't know me," I said, "You don't know how long winded I can be! You sure you want to give me the floor?" I joked.

"Yes!" The group said, again in unison as everyone smiled. The group understood "talkers" and welcomed the stories, whether long and detailed or short and concise. Sharing my story is one way that has helped me remain strong in my recovery through the years.

I didn't have time to share my whole testimony that night. I only spoke for ten minutes. In all honesty, it would have taken hours, maybe days, to share my whole story. So here I am, sharing my story of recovery with you. I hope my story will be both a challenge and an inspiration to every reader, whether in recovery or not.

Everyone's experience in life is different. Every story is different; however, we have much in common in the fact that we all can be freed from whatever has us bound. We can overcome the darkest of choices and consequences.

Mine is a story of hard times, but it is also a story of hope, healing and victory. It is the truth about my life on the street, and the reality of my HIV diagnosis, but it is also the truth about my redemption despite it all. It is my journey from a world void of light to a new world full of light, free from addiction and in recovery.

For me life began on March 12, 1979; I was born in Ocala, Florida, to Joseph and Diana, two sailors in the U.S. Navy. With my birth, my mother received an honorable discharge from military service and became a stay-at-home mom. It wasn't long until my parents divorced. Their marriage was already in trouble, and the addition of a baby did not help. A custody battle ensued, eventually resulting with my dad receiving full custody. Dad was my hero. He left the Navy to raise me.

We lived in central Louisiana near my dad's family, where he worked a minimum wage job. Eventually, he married a woman he worked with named Crystal, and we moved to Texas for three years. Shortly after our move, my baby sister Alicia was born. I was so excited to have a little sister; I adored her!

Our life wasn't perfect at home. Crystal had anger problems and was verbally abusive to me. In turn, I was very rebellious. We argued everyday. Crystal always apologized when her anger was out of control, and I felt sorry for her because I knew she had problems and suffered from mental illness.

Finally, Dad and Crystal made the decision to divorce and we all moved to Central Louisiana near family. Alicia stayed with Crystal, and Dad and I moved in with his parents. I was in fourth grade and things were great. I was happy living with my grandparents; they were very safe and kind people. I made many fun memories during that time. Living with my grandparents was the best time of my childhood.

Even though Dad had full custody of me, Mom was still very much a part of my life. Every holiday she sent me a package full of expensive gifts. Three times a year, I went to South Florida to see her. One visit, I arrived at the airport and Mom was there with a limousine waiting for me. We rode all over town in the limousine, shopping for new, trendy clothes. On other visits, we went to places like the beach and Disney World. The summer before I started fifth grade, Mom took me to my first rock concert—Tom Petty and the Heartbreakers. Dad wasn't too happy about the trip to the concert because I was only ten years old.

It was the 80s and Mom remarried a guy named Cliff. They lived in South Florida and constantly hosted big parties at their house. Mom was a hair stylist and Cliff was an electrician. Cliff was also an addict. The addiction was a major source of argument between Cliff and Mom. As a child, I didn't know what an addict was. All I remember is that I got along well with my step-dad; we had a special bond. I loved being at their house. I loved the excitement of the parties. At the time I didn't know where all their money came from, but looking back I think it probably had something to do with the drugs. Then, suddenly it all came to an end. There was another divorce and my life changed again.

When I went to visit Mom after the divorce, I stayed with my Aunt Jan while Mom was at work. Aunt Jan and I became close; we still are. I vented to her anytime I was upset. She was the one who encouraged me on a spiritual level, sharing scriptures and Bible principles with me. If I was mad about something, she reminded me, "The Bible says we have to forgive. Here it is in Matthew 6:14-15, "For if ye forgive men their trespasses, your heavenly Father will also forgive you: But if ye forgive not men their trespasses, neither will your Father forgive your trespasses."

Mom ended up marrying again, this time to a man named Stanley. He really loved her and had his own business. Stanley was a good man, and was not an addict. He was great for my mom. He was a positive influence that made my mom a better person.

The summer before fifth grade when I came back to my dad's from Florida, I was in for a shock. Dad and Crystal were back together, and their lifestyle was changing into something I had never known.

"We started going to church, and we really like it," Crystal explained.

"We think you will like it too," Dad added.

When I visited the church for the first time my only thought was, "Whatever this is, it is not really a church."

I was used to more traditional services full of respectful silence. Dad and Crystal's church was loud and boisterous. The sound of drums and other musical instruments filled the air with exuberant music. People stood clapping and raising their hands. Some people even danced. They looked like they were having so much fun! I learned later that all of the excitement was their way of worshipping God.

Dad was right; I did like the church. It seemed like our family changed overnight. Dad and Crystal were back together, I had a little sister again and we were happy. It was great. The church was interesting, different and fun. During services, we sat at the back where I watched everyone and everything. I couldn't believe what I heard and saw. The choir was the most amazing thing in the world. I loved it. "When I grow up, I'm going to sing in the choir," I insisted.

Eventually, all of us decided to be baptized. My dad also joined a group committed to extra times of prayer. He regularly went to the church to pray. As a family we often went to Bible studies, and some nights we stayed up praying until one and two in the morning. We were also a part of the church Easter play, which I really enjoyed.

What we did and said outside of church changed too. The way we dressed, the words we used, and the entertainment we enjoyed was wholesome. I took my Bible to school with me and read it during recess while the other children played. I was a regular church girl! I loved church, and I loved my new life.

The only thing I was disappointed about was that I had not yet experienced the Biblical promise of receiving the gift of the Holy Ghost the way that many of the other kids at church had. I kept hearing preaching about Acts 2:38, "Then Peter said unto them, repent and be baptized every one of you in the name of Jesus Christ, and ye shall receive the gift of the Holy Ghost." The Holy Ghost is God's Spirit.

"What's wrong with me?" I asked God as I prayed. "All the other kids are speaking in tongues, but not me. I want the Holy Ghost so much." I didn't get my answer, but I kept praying and reading my Bible.

After six weeks of consistently praying, one Wednesday night at children's church, I could feel the love of God all around me so strongly it nearly took my breath away. I asked God to come and live in my heart and to fill me with His love. As I was praying, my lips began to tremble and I started speaking in a language I had never learned as God filled me with His Spirit. I spoke in tongues for such a long time that my voice became hoarse! I was so excited about God and what was happening in my life! I was ten years old.

Despite how great I felt when I received the Holy Ghost, I had my own childhood battles to face. In sixth grade, no one asked me to go to the school dance. I remember feeling upset and rejected. After school one evening, I was in my bedroom and started praying: "Jesus, nobody wants to dance with me. Nobody even asked me to the dance. Will you dance with me?"

God once again poured His love on me that night. I danced all over the room worshipping Jesus, and started speaking in tongues. His Spirit was so strong in the room, it was as if we were holding hands and He was guiding me in a personal, spiritual dance. I could feel the love of

God all over me. All of the feelings of rejection and pain melted away when I turned to God. He understood me and loved me as I was. That was a very serious, spiritual experience for me. My faith was alive, and I believed there was nothing that God couldn't do.

Another Wednesday night in children's church, there was a skit that I will never forget. Some teenagers were dressed up as demons; others were dressed up like angels. The angels ran in and started fighting the demons. As I watched the dramatization, I felt the Spirit of God building my faith. I jumped up out of my chair and started speaking in tongues, crying with a loud voice.

A teacher came up to me while I was praying. She told me to put my hand on the shoulder of the kid next to me. When I touched the girl's shoulder, she jumped up and started speaking in tongues with a loud voice, just like me. When that girl touched the next kid it happened again. It was like a Holy Ghost domino effect. Everyone was praying in tongues. The love and power of God was so strong in that room. It was an amazing night, and I remember it vividly to this day!

Outside of church, my life wasn't going so great. Physically and emotionally, I had all the issues of most normal adolescent girls. My face was always broken out, and I developed a nervous habit of picking at my face, which made it worse. I was called "zit-face" and "zit-girl" at school. None of the boys liked me and very few of the girls liked me.

My life was very unbalanced. I wanted to pray and read my Bible all the time; I didn't want to do my schoolwork. I had difficulty concentrating. I couldn't seem to focus on any one thing. I was perpetually distracted. My grades started failing, and I ended up forced to repeat sixth grade. It was my parents' decision that my second chance at sixth grade should be in private school. At my new school the other kids made fun of me, not only because of my zits, but for my religious beliefs as well. Despite the bullying, I passed sixth grade and for seventh grade I returned to the public junior high my church friends attended.

In seventh grade, I was more interested in my social life at church than I was interested in my relationship with God. I went from being overly spiritual to just wanting to hang out with friends. Most of my friends had the same mentality I did, but I did have one friend who was spiritually minded. In seventh grade, we often met in a little hallway in between class and prayed for our teachers and the other students. This was my one public acknowledgement of the power of prayer that in my heart I still deeply believed in.

My life at home was as out of balance as I was. Even though our family went to church and stayed involved in activities, Dad and Crystal still constantly argued. They became lax in their church attendance. I hated it when they slept in on Sunday mornings instead of going to church. On those mornings, I isolated myself in my room and tried to pray and read my Bible.

I was very afraid when I was at home because of the emotional drama and strife that was a part of my home life. Crystal belittled me and called me names everyday. If I did something wrong, I lied about it because I was afraid of punishment. I stayed in my room and out of the way as much as I could.

I didn't like to be alone, and I didn't like to be at home, so many mornings I left for school an hour early. I had a church friend who lived near our school and I went to her house at 7 a.m. She was my best friend, and her family never seemed to mind the early-morning intrusion. I felt safe at church and at school, and I was in the choir at both places. I loved to sing; it made me feel at peace. Sometimes singing the songs at home brought peace to my heart when I was troubled by family problems.

My dad did everything he could to make things fun for our family. I remember a vacation we took to Hot Springs, Arkansas where Dad rented a pontoon houseboat. We also visited a wax museum and I remember playing miniature golf with him. I had so much fun!

No matter how hard Dad tried to make things work for our family, my relationship with Crystal was a nightmare. We simply could not stand each other. When I found out that I would be considered an adult at age eighteen, I made up my mind I would move out on my own no matter what.

As it turned out, Crystal wanted me to move out immediately. "I want you to move in with your mom," she said to me after an argument one day. "If you don't, I'm going to divorce your dad and it will be all your fault for breaking up the family!"

I went to my dad, who worked at the local fire department, and asked if I could move to Florida to see what life was like living with my mom. I never told him what Crystal said to me because I was so intimidated by her. I moved during my eighth grade year.

South Florida

When I arrived in South Florida, I was unexpectedly at a loss. I left all of my friends and my church in Louisiana, and moved in with a mother who was an unbeliever. Mom took me to church two or three times when I first moved in. I was not allowed to talk about God at home. It was okay for me to read my Bible alone in my room, but I was to keep it to myself. Prayer that anyone could hear was out of the question.

Mom was sensitive to how I felt after the move and about the spiritual conflicts we had, so she spent special mother-daughter time with me each week to help build our relationship. We often went to the bookstore and enjoyed coffee and deserts together while browsing interesting books.

Mom and Stanley loved to travel, and I was blessed they took me with them. We went to Europe where we visited France, Brussels, Luxembourg, and the Netherlands. I remember seeing the Eiffel Tower in Paris and eating chocolate filled croissants for breakfast. I had so much fun. At one point on the trip we were at a German restaurant and I remember thinking if I spoke English really loud and slow, the staff would understand me. My family laughed at how silly I was.

After our European trip, Mom took us on a trip to Arizona. I stood on a high cliff looking over the Grand Canyon. Looking over the canyon moved me to tears. The overwhelming beauty of nature reminded me of how great God was as Creator. I thanked Him silently for His magnificent artwork.

While living with my mom, I attended the local middle school where I was considered a minority. Most students at school were Latino. I looked like, talked like, and dressed like a southern church girl, which garnered quite a bit of attention. It seemed like all the kids made fun of me for one thing or another. No one understood me, or my faith. I simply didn't fit in at all, anywhere. As a result, I became severely depressed. I started overeating. I would drink a six-pack of sodas every night. I started gaining weight and feeling even worse about myself than ever. My teenage self-esteem was spiraling downward.

I felt angry toward God. In my mind God didn't love me, and didn't care that I moved to a place where I had no friends. I felt rejected and depressed. I didn't practice my faith any more. I felt that if God didn't care, why should I try?

I was not happy and my behavior reflected my frustration. I started skipping school and buying diet pills from the pharmacy; I hid it all from my mom. I had a myriad of emotional problems—some were normal to adolescents and others more severe. I became overly dependent on anyone who showed me attention, taking them emotionally hostage through manipulation. I didn't know what it meant to have a healthy friendship. I longed for a spiritual and emotional connection with my mom, and looked to other people to fill that role. It was a period of time in my life when I cried all of the time.

Finally an opportunity came my way that gave me hope for a happier life in Florida. I had one talent that I believed in, my ability to sing. I applied to a high school for talented kids. Students had to have a high grade point average and audition to be considered. I spent hours singing with my middle school choir teacher, until it was finally the day of the audition. The line to the dark audition room wrapped around the door and down the hallway. I wore a special outfit my mom bought me and waited patiently.

It was finally my turn. The judges sat at a table facing the stage. My stomach was in knots. As I began to sing, suddenly my mind went blank. I forgot the words—that had never happened to me before. I didn't make the cut. It devastated me.

I started ninth grade at a public high school known for its athletic program. Sports didn't interest me, but I did join the choir. I finally made friends at school by agreeing to do their homework and by buying them gifts. One day, my friends came into the choir room laughing hysterically. I want to be that happy, I thought as I watched them giggling. I walked up to them and said, "Did something funny happen?"

"We're trippin'," one of them said. "It's a hit of acid."

"How much is it and where can I get some?" I wanted to try it because I wanted to be happy like they were.

"Go to the park next to the high school and look for the hippies selling incense," one of the kids told me. "Ask for an Alice in Wonderland."

I went and found the hippie kids. I bought a hit and they handed me a little piece of cloth about the size of a stamp that was dipped in acid. I put the cloth on my tongue and the chemicals began to dissolve in my mouth. Not long after the high began, I fell in love with acid.

At that time, a hit was $5. Mom gave me $5 a day for lunch and $25 a week for doing chores. My mom gave me more money than my friends' parents gave them, so I saved money and bought hits for me and my friends each week. We'd skip school and get high. At last I was laughing again.

Some of my friends were also smoking pot, and I decided to try it. Since I had never smoked even a cigarette, I didn't know exactly how to inhale while smoking a joint. My friends were eager to teach me. Later, I started smoking cigarettes as well.

When the high was over, and reality set in, I always felt really depressed. I knew everything I was doing was wrong. My life was full of lies and deception. My coping mechanism was simply to get high again and not have to deal with reality and my guilt for using drugs.

As most high school students do, my friends and I exchanged notes during class. Of course, we often referred to drugs. Mom discovered one of the notes and freaked out. Three days later I was on a plane returning to my father in Louisiana, far away from access to my friends and their ready suppliers of acid and pot.

Central Louisiana

When I arrived back in Louisiana, life was nothing like it was two years before when I left for Florida. My dad and Crystal didn't go to church at all; they hadn't in a long time. My baby brother Alan was born while I was away and it was cool to have a little brother. He was very sweet and easy to love. I enjoyed helping take care of him.

The beginning of my tenth grade year, Dad and Crystal thought it was a good idea for me join an extra-curricular school activity. "It would help you make friends," Dad said.

"You should be a Booster!" Crystal said. "That's a lot of fun!"

Being a Booster was the stepping-stone toward being a cheerleader, or on the dance line, and though I had aspirations for neither, I joined and actually had fun participating in the various activities.

Later that year, Crystal drove me to tryouts for the school play. Drama was something I was interested in. I was selected to be a part of a singing group. I practiced everyday. I was prepared, but once again stage fright got the best of me.

"I don't want to do this anymore," I said to Dad and Crystal.

"What? We've taken you to all these practices and you've done so well. Why don't you want to be involved?" They asked.

I didn't have an answer. Inside, I was afraid of failure and making a fool of myself. I didn't want to be humiliated by forgetting my part again, like I did in the audition a year ago. On the day of the production I sat in the crowd and watched. All I could think was, "What have I done? I could have been a part of the play, but I dropped out because of fear." I was still a Booster, but I felt like a failure and was self-conscious about dropping out of the play.

I was self-conscious in other areas of my life too, especially about my looks. I was paranoid about the acne on my face, and I started picking my skin again. I was obsessed. I would pick at my face and any area of my body that had a bump, scratch, or blemish. I picked for hours and made each spot bleed. Now I had a new problem—scabs.

"How do I hide all of the scabs?" I thought. I started wearing long pants and long-sleeves all of the time. Try being a Booster during Louisiana's seasons, wearing booster sweatpants under a booster skirt, and a booster sweatshirt over a booster top. I was dressed the way the other girls would dress for winter, but it was spring and fall. If I didn't wear all of those clothes, my secret would be revealed. Underneath all the layers, I looked like I had the chickenpox!

I didn't give anyone a straight answer about my clothes. I hid my problem from everyone, as if I had a secret life. I didn't know what was wrong with me and I didn't know how to explain my problem. All I knew was that I felt very different from everyone else my age. I spent my time after school alone in the bathroom searching my skin for imperfections. I didn't give my skin a chance to heal. For me, skin picking was an addiction.

Despite my issues, I still had to go to school. I was in a speech class that year, the only sophomore in a class full of seniors. Every Friday I gave a speech to the class, and I aced every speech. I loved giving speeches; I was a natural at it. At that point in my life I wanted to be a psychologist, so every week I studied a different mental illness and gave a speech about it. Maybe it was studying psychology that opened my eyes to some of my issues. I knew I needed help. I was experiencing extreme mood swings, going from severely happy to severely sad. My skin-picking problem kept me too busy to watch TV, hang out with friends, or do anything relaxing. I decided it was time to intervene in my own life.

Even though Crystal was an angry person, she did have a soft motherly side to her, so I decided to go to her for help. "I need to show you something in the bathroom," I said.

Crystal looked at me puzzled. We went to the bathroom and I started taking off my clothes to show Crystal my skin. She looked at me and started crying. "Baby, we are going to get you some help," she said.

I went to school the next morning and was called out of class in the middle of the day. Crystal had come to pick me up. "We are putting you in the hospital," she said. She talked to a doctor earlier that day, and put his advice into action immediately.

The hospital staff recognized my emotional highs and lows. I was excited and talked for hours, then all of a sudden I was depressed—sure signs of Bipolar Disorder. I was diagnosed with Bipolar Disorder, also called Manic Depressive Disorder and Obsessive Compulsive Disorder (OCD) and put on medication for both.

I had to read books on Bipolar Disorder and OCD. I also had to make changes at home. The doctors advised my parents to cover or take down all of the mirrors. I was not allowed to have long nails. I had to wear gloves to prohibit me from picking at any bumps I might find. I lived out the rest of my high school years in a state of heavy medication. I was neither happy, nor sad. I lived in the numb emotional state because of the medication. It bothered me that I didn't feel joy or sorrow. I was tired all of the time. I felt nothing.

Making friends was difficult, but I did develop a few friendships. I became best friends with a girl named Cindi. She just happened to smoke pot. We did a lot of typical high school girl stuff, but we added pot to the mix. And with me, the mix included the already high levels of medication prescribed by my doctors.

One night, I was staying at Cindi's house and we went outside to walk around her neighborhood and smoke pot. We came back to her house and the door was locked. We rang the bell. Her mom answered the door.

"Cindi? Angelena?" Cindi's mom asked in a deep southern accent. "What do you two girls think yer doin' comin' up in my house lookin' all bug-eyed?" We could hardly contain our laughter.

Cindi was a smart girl. She was going places in her life, despite the pot. She was determined to have a good life. There were certain things she wouldn't do that the rest of our crowd did. I did everything! Our group of friends constantly partied. We smoked cigarettes. We smoked pot. We skipped school, sometimes just a class and sometimes all day.

One day during my junior year, I brought a bag of weed with me to school. I planned to split it with some of the other kids. I was nervous because I had never actually brought pot to school with me before. I had a very uneasy feeling all morning. Finally, I asked for a pass to leave my classroom. I went to the restroom and flushed the weed down the toilet.

Shortly after I came back to my class, the principal and two other administrators showed up and requested that I bring my belongings and come with them. The principal explained that they had reason to search my bags. They found my cigarettes and my lighter, but no marijuana. I was suspended for three days. I feel certain one of my friends turned me in, but I never found out who ratted me out.

The rest of high school, my grades continued to drop. I did only what I had to do to graduate. I was in and out of the mental hospital each year. I was on all kinds of medications, and, of course, I continued to smoke pot. I was absent more than I was present in class. I was constantly in and out of dope houses. I surrounded myself with guys getting loaded and drunk. I became romantically involved with one of the guys.

On my eighteenth birthday, in March of my senior year of high school, my emancipation day finally arrived. I went to the kitchen, grabbed several black garbage bags, and packed my belongings. I loaded the garbage bags into my car. I left my dad's house and drove to a friend's place. My stay there was not long; her parents kicked me out shortly after I moved in. I went to another friend's house, but again the parents were not tolerant of my drugs or behaviors. I dropped out of high school just weeks before graduation. To get money for drugs, I went with my guy friends to give blood. We earned $20 every other week for giving blood. We pooled our funds, bought drugs and stayed high for as long as we could.

One day, we came up with the fabulous idea to party in a city about an hour away. We loaded my car with alcohol and drugs. I was too high to drive, so I handed the keys to one of my friends. I was in the backseat with two guys. We arrived at another friend's house and stayed for almost two weeks. We ran out of money and gas. Someone slashed my tires. The guys and I walked to a local shelter to eat lunch everyday. Someone felt sorry for us since we were stuck so far from home, so they gave me spare tires and gas, and we were able to make the trip back home.

I dropped a couple of the guys off at their respective houses. The rest of us decided to stop at one of the other guy's homes. His parents weren't home, and we piled in the living room. My boyfriend broke up with me right there in front of everyone. He told me it was over and suggested I go back home to my parents. I loved him, but he didn't return the love. I was humiliated in front of my friends.

"You are on a downward spiral," one of my friends said.

I was in denial. I immediately started crying and ran to my car. My parents' house was not an option, regardless of his suggestion, so I went to another friend's house. I was there a few nights before my dad showed up.

"Give me the keys to the car," he said. "That car is in my name. If this is the way you want to live your life, then have a nice life." He took the keys, turned around and walked out the door.

I was now both homeless and car-less. All of my friends tried to talk me into going home, making peace with my family, and getting my life together. I didn't want to go home, but I didn't have another option. I finally did go, but my family didn't know what to do with me.

Dad and Crystal and Mom and Stanley decided I should move back to South Florida to start my life over. My mom and step-dad said they would help me get on my feet financially. They flew to Louisiana to pick me up. The plan was to put me on Medicaid and Medicare for my legitimate medications and health needs. A renewed commitment to treatment should get me balanced and working. I agreed and took off to Florida to start my new and productive life.

When we arrived in Florida, my mom gave me a to-do list. I had one year to earn my GED, get a job, buy a car and rent an apartment. I lived with Mom and Stanley while I pulled my life back together. My mom said, "Angel, we will help you with all of this, but once the year is up and these things are accomplished, you're out. You're a grown-up now." At first, Mom and Stanley drove me everywhere I needed to go. That got old pretty quick and it wasn't long before they bought me a used car.

I completed my GED and started working at a department store during the day and at a restaurant at night. I took my medicine, and I went to a counselor every other week. I found a great apartment. My parents took care of the first month's rent and bought me everything I needed. I was out of their house in less than a year.

From Louisiana, family news came from Crystal. "You have a new baby sister! Her name is Alyssa, and she is beautiful!" Life was going on for them without me. I was just getting started on a new life of my own, independent from both sets of parents. With that freedom, came responsibility and more choices to make.

I became involved with a nice guy named Ted. I worked with his sister at the department store. She thought I was great, so she set us up. Ted was half Irish and half Cuban. He was a quiet, handsome college student. Ted was over six feet tall, and towered over my less than five-foot frame. He had goals and he worked diligently to achieve them.

His life was on the right track. For the first time in a long time, my life seemed to be on track too.

After a couple of months, I invited Ted to meet my parents. My Mom and Stanley decided it was the perfect opportunity to play a joke on Ted. They typed up some questions to use while they interviewed him about dating their daughter. We knocked on the front door. My mom greeted us in her bathrobe and invited us inside. My stepdad came out dressed in leather and chains, fitting because he owned a motorcycle shop.

"Before the two of you leave tonight, I have some questions I need to ask," Mom said to Ted. She pulled out the list of questions and clicked her pen. "Have you ever been arrested? Have you been married? Do you have kids? Are you in college? What was the reason for your last breakup? Are you willing to submit to a background check?" She rattled off.

The look on Ted's face was well worth the effort they put into the practical joke. After about ten minutes, they finally told him they were kidding. It was hilarious!

Ted was sweet, kind, and generous. He was good in every kind of way. My parents loved Ted. Ted loved me. He was good for me, and underneath it all, I hated it. I was not attracted to him because he was just too nice.

Later, Mom and Stanley were planning a weekend trip to the Bahamas, and invited Ted and me to come along. We went to the Bahamas, but no one knew how I really felt about Ted. I knew I had to tell him the truth. Before we left the islands, I took Ted to a bar, got him buzzed and broke up with him. I told him when we got back to Florida I didn't want to see him again. I broke his heart when I told him I wasn't into him like he was into me. He was devastated; I was free.

Shortly after returning home from our trip, my doctors decided they needed to change my medicine. I once again found myself in the hospital for treatment. While there, I saw the most beautiful man I'd ever seen. I made sure to introduce myself to him. He was so very good looking, but he seemed kind of quiet. I knew I was at a psychiatric hospital and the man could be there for any number of reasons; however, I told myself that maybe he was just there for something simple and treatable, like depression.

His name was Donny. We became friends and decided that after we left the hospital, we would continue our relationship. We started dating and it wasn't too long before I noticed Donny had some ways about him that weren't quite right. Every time Donny saw me, and I mean every time, he gave me a used stuffed animal from his bedroom. His room was full of old stuffed animals, as if people gave him stuffed animals for gifts all of the time.

One day, Donny came over to visit me. We were in my room talking when we started arguing. Donny got very angry. He started picking up the stuffed animals he had given me and throwing them at me. He was extremely mad. I looked at him and calmly said, "Donny, it's over."

"What?" He asked, stuffed animal in hand, poised to hurl at me.

"It's over," I repeated. At that moment Donny began to cuss and throw even more of his old stuffed animals at me.

I realized that the differences between us were irreconcilable, but a part of me still liked him. Upset over the breakup, I went to my mom's house to find some comfort for my broken heart.

"Now Angel," Mom said, "What did you really think you'd get when you found this guy at a psychiatric hospital?" Let's just say this experience helped me decide not to pick up men at the hospital again.

I decided I needed a change of scenery. It was time to get a new job. I met a girl who told me about a full-time job at a barbecue restaurant. I started working as a cashier, earning a salary of $100 a week, plus tips. It was at the barbecue restaurant where I reconnected to the drug world.

I bought a hit of acid from a guy named Alex. We exchanged numbers, and it wasn't long before I fell for him. After all, he was the most beautiful man I had ever seen. He had a full-time job. Unlike Donny, he was a real man—there were no stuffed animals in his bedroom.

Alex wasn't perfect, but I thought he was perfect for me. He had real problems in his life, but I knew I could love him enough to fix them. I knew my love for him was so strong it would move both of us from a lifestyle of drugs and alcohol into a pure and drug-free relationship.

I had no boundaries with Alex. I spent $100 a week on pot for us to share. Our relationship consisted of getting high and sleeping together. I soon learned though, Alex was a player. He wanted an open relationship. I agreed; I did anything in order to keep him in my life.

I lost all my friends because of my relationship with Alex. He slept with my friends when they were high or drunk, and I blamed the girls. I cut them out of my life, yet I stayed with Alex. I didn't hold him responsible at all.

I was addicted to Alex. He was my idol. I used every form of manipulation to keep him in my life, even though he was verbally abusive. I forgave him each time he treated me wrongly. I had such low self-esteem I truly believed I needed to work hard to keep him because no other man would love me like he loved me.

The relationship meant everything to me, but it meant nothing to him. Alex refused to be seen in public with me. He didn't even let me take his picture. Yet, in my twisted mind and heart, I truly thought he was the man I was going to marry. I believed one day he would come to his senses. I was going to be the girl that stood by his side while he went through his process of change. It didn't work. As time went on, I realized I was not able to control him. He wasn't changing for the better. He was changing for the worse.

My relationship with Alex led me to prostitution. He told me his boss would pay to sleep with me. It was a way I could get more money for drugs for both of us. Alex arranged for us to meet. As planned, we used the money I made from his boss to pay for drugs. I met his boss once a week for an hour and made $100. That was the first time I used my body to make money.

It wasn't long before I found more men who paid me to sleep with them. I met four different men each week, and made so much money I quit my job at the restaurant. Along with the money, the men told me I was pretty. I was not used to anyone saying anything positive about me, and it made me feel good.

My relationship with Alex lasted almost a year. It was the unhealthiest relationship I ever had. While he was never physically abusive, he verbally and emotionally abused me. Alex knew that I loved him and used that as a weapon to manipulate me to act in ways I never had before. Alex knew I was loyal and wouldn't break up with him.

For Christmas, I bought him two Polo shirts and had them gift-wrapped. While on my way to celebrate the holidays with my parents, I stopped by Alex's house to give him his gift. When I pulled up in the driveway, he came out to meet me. He didn't let me into the house. He pulled out the key to my apartment, handed it to me and said, "Angel, all this is over."

I felt my heart drop. I was in a state of shock—horrified and devastated. I drove to my apartment and with shaking hands lit a cigarette. When I walked in the door, I didn't even bother to make sure it completely shut. I fell to the floor and started crying hysterically. I was hurt and frustrated. My plan to keep Alex did not work. What was I going to do now? I was mad at myself for loving him even though I knew he was using me. Why did I fall for this type of man? It was my choice to love Alex that ended up crushing my own heart.

A neighbor, a supposed friend of mine, heard me crying. She came to my apartment to console me. She acted like she cared and was kind, but I knew she was sleeping with Alex and again, I was angry with her, not him. I got up off the floor and told her to get out of my place and never come back again.

I finally pulled myself together enough to go to my family's gathering. I told my family Alex and I broke up. I hoped to find sympathy and support for my broken heart, but it didn't happen. They were happy he was out of my life. I was alone in my misery.

The breakup was a traumatic crisis for me. I decided to get high to cope. I wasn't the same after Alex. The whole relationship hardened me. It changed how I thought about men. Men became nothing but objects to me, a source of money. I promised myself I would never let anyone hurt me like Alex hurt me, ever again.

On my way home after leaving my family, I didn't care what happened next in my life. I counted the money I received in gifts. I had a total of $400 in cash. I stopped at a gas station, bought a carton of cigarettes and filled up my car with gas. I turned the radio on and cried, driving aimlessly about thirty miles to a different part of the city.

I pulled into another gas station. I saw a rough looking man standing outside. I had never seen the man before, but I had a feeling he could tell me where to find drugs. I rolled down my window and called to the man.

"Look, I have enough money right now to take care of me and you. Just bring me to a place where I can find some dope," I said. He hopped in the car and directed me to a house about ten minutes away. Finally, I thought, a place to get high. We parked in front of a rundown house, walked up the steps, and the man I was with opened the door. I could see inside the living room from where I stood; it was full of men sitting around on couches.

I walked into the house. There was a very tangible presence of darkness all around me. I could feel the demonic spirits. I knew I was in the presence of evil.

"I want $100 worth of dope," I said as I sat down with the men. A young man took my $100, hopped on a bicycle and left. He was back in fifteen minutes with crack cocaine, not marijuana as I had expected. Each of the men in the room pulled out a glass pipe.

"Show me how to smoke it," I said. My heart was broken; I wanted to get high. I didn't care what type of drug it was. They showed me, and I smoked it.

I didn't realize I could become addicted to crack cocaine overnight. I thought I could smoke it one time and be done with it, as I did with marijuana. I went through the rest of my $400 that night smoking crack until the sun came up. I walked in the room knowing very little about crack cocaine; I walked out of the room an addict. Within a few months, my entire life revolved around cocaine addiction.

Life on the street was dirty. The culture was dirty, the language was dirty, the

people were dirty, and the spirits were dirty. I learned a lot living on the street—a lot I wish I didn't know, a lot I wish I could forget.

I learned what "feening" and "jonesing" felt like. It's the feeling of anxiety that raged and screamed through my body, "I've just got to have a hit!"

Something else I learned on the street: people who smoke crack make their own crack pipes. A crack pipe is often called a "rose" or a "stem" because among the parts required to make the pipe is a small glass tube usually sold in gas stations and convenience stores. The tube usually is home to a man-made rose, and keeps the stem of the rose straight. The rose in a tube is supposed to be a thoughtful gift; not thrown aside to use the meaningless tube for smoking crack. Like all things, an innocent trinket can be distorted and used for evil.

On each end of the tube is a small round cover. I took the cover off of one end, held the glass tube up, and blew a puff of air that shot the rose out across the room. Next, I'd take a charbroil, an orange scrub that people normally use to clean their kitchen sink, rip a small piece off of it, roll the piece and stick it in the end of the tube. I lit the piece of charbroil to burn it, so it would not taste so bad. It made a sort of filter that filled up about an inch of the pipe. I put the crack rock on the piece of charbroil.

As I smoked the pipe, the end of the glass tube began to crack because of the heat. As pieces of pipe broke off,

I'd push the charbroil filter further up the pipe. Then, I'd turn the pipe around to continue smoking. I'd use the pipe until it was almost totally broken off.

Crack pipes were in high demand. It was very common for people to share their pipes. It was also common for people to fight over crack pipes. Jessica, a good friend of mine, went into a rage if she lost her crack pipe. When she was feening and couldn't find her own pipe, she was quick to take someone else's. Women addicted to crack often hid their drugs and their pipes in their bras. Men hid their crack rocks in baggies in their mouths.

Many people do not realize sharing crack pipes is one way Hepatitis is spread. When a person infected with Hepatitis smokes the broken end of a crack pipe, their lips may be burned or cut by the pipe. Then, when they share their pipe with someone else, infected blood spreads Hepatitis to the next user. As is the case with most crack addicts, when I smoked crack, I never thought about my health. All I thought about was getting my next high.

Crack pipes, drugs and other drug paraphernalia are all a daily part of street life. HIV, AIDS, and other sexually transmitted diseases are also part of the norm. I knew a lot of people with STDs, so to me it didn't seem like a death sentence; it was normal. When I was in South Florida, I met a lot of people with HIV and AIDS, and they seemed fine to me. I once had a counselor who lived with HIV for over 20 years. People who don't know anything about HIV or AIDS often think the person has two years to live, a misconception based on medical reports from the 1980s when medication was not as advanced as it is now.

Currently, a person can live with HIV up to 50 years, as long as they are consistently on medication. Many people, driven by either pride or denial or both, that do not want to acknowledge they could have something like HIV, do not get tested for it even though they are at risk. The virus spreads because many don't even know they are infected. Despite risky behavior, some refuse HIV testing, but refusing to face the truth does not change the truth. Undergoing HIV testing shows strong personal responsibility for the health and wellbeing of self and others.

Life on the street was dangerous. It was dark and full of sin. My life on the street taught me a lot about people. I learned very quickly to trust no one. Street life was all about me taking care of me. Everyone manipulated each other to feed their own addictions. People on the street were motivated by selfish desires. They didn't care about hanging out, being friends, or helping each other find a better life.

There was a crack dealer named Sean whom I considered a friend. It was easy for me to get into a relationship with him that was not emotional, but completely drug related. He somewhat cared for me, but I used him the whole time as my source for a constant supply of crack.

"I have a friend in the hospital who is dying of AIDS," Sean said to me one day. "I want you to come with me to visit him." I agreed and off we went.

When we walked through the door to the man's hospital room, the man began to beg us to help him leave the hospital. "Please, please don't let me die here. I don't want to die in a hospital room by myself. I want to die how I lived," he said.

It made sense to me. He was an obvious crack addict with no family to support him. His dying wish was to die high; he wanted to end his life loaded. I honestly felt like it didn't matter if the man stayed in the hospital or not. He had his mind made up and his life was ending either way.

I saw the man again a couple of days later in a crack house. He was smoking crack, lying on a mattress placed straight on the concrete floor. The room was empty except for a single light bulb that hung down over the mattress on a wire. A few days later, the man died. It didn't bother anyone that the man died alone.

Like everyone else on the street, I lived my life to get my next high and to protect myself as much as possible. I ran into a lot of situations that were very dangerous. I began having seizures while I was living on the street. The first time I had a seizure I was at a crack house with a bunch of other people. I was smoking and started inhaling as much as I could. I must have blacked out. All I remember is sitting up and looking around.

"Where's my pipe?" I asked with accusation in my voice. "Someone took my pipe."

The room was full of men staring at me. Some of them had worried looks on their faces. The owner of the house came to where I was. "You just had a seizure," he said. "You turned blue."

I didn't believe him. "I don't have seizures," I said defensively.

"Look at the clock!" The man insisted. "You've been out for 20 minutes! There is blood all around your mouth!"

"No, there isn't!" I was in complete denial.

He picked up a mirror and held it up to my face. I was pale, with dried blood around my mouth. "Leave," he said. "I'm not selling to you any more. I can't have stuff like that happening here. If the cops and ambulances have to come here, we'll all get busted. You're out!"

I left with the dried blood all around my mouth. I went home, took a wet washcloth, wiped the blood off, put red lip-stick on, and went back out to turn a trick—sell myself—so I get more crack and get high. I was so addicted I didn't think about taking care of myself.

Another time, I walked through a park in a bad neighborhood looking for a runner to bring me some crack. Runners make their money by running to the dope house and bringing the dope back to the buyer. The buyer usually breaks off a piece of crack for the runner as payment. I found someone who agreed to go to the dealer for me. I decided to smoke the rest of my crack while I waited at the park for the runner to return. I took a big hit. It wasn't long before my body started shaking. It was another seizure, and this time I was fully alert.

I watched my pipe fly out of my hands as I started shaking. My body fell to the ground; I was completely out of control. I was conscious enough to know I was on the ground flipping around. All I could think of was, I hope no one is seeing this. They will never sell to me in this neighborhood again.

As soon as my body calmed down, I looked around. I didn't see anyone. It didn't appear that anyone had seen my episode. I found my pipe and lighter a few feet away from where I fell. The runner came back with more drugs; I paid him and continued to smoke.

Even seizures weren't enough to turn me off of crack. My life was not important. My health was of no concern to me. The only thing I cared about was the crack. Crack caused me to put myself in danger, multiple times. Not only did I risk my health with the drugs, I risked it with the people I was associated with. I risked it living on the streets. Looking back, I can see how God spared my life many times.

I will never forget the most dangerous experience I ever had. I was alone on the street. That particular night, I was walking with crack hidden in my clothes. Several police cars surrounded me. The cops searched my purse. There wasn't a female cop, so they didn't body search me, and didn't find my drugs.

"Get off the street," they demanded.

I went on my way. I walked down the road and rounded the corner. Ahead of me stood several drug dealers and prostitutes. I called out to warn them of the danger nearby. "There's blue lights around the corner!"

People started scattering everywhere, going into buildings, and getting off the street. I saw a drug dealer I recognized. I never bought crack from him because there was something about him I didn't trust, but tonight I needed his assistance.

"Hey," I called out to the man, "I don't need to buy anything from you, I have all I need, but could you take me to a place where I can get away from the cops and get high?" He nodded his head "yes," and I followed after him as we ran to his house.

There was no electricity in the house. It was dark, the windows were boarded up and a small beam from the streetlight shined through cracks between the boards. I followed the man into his bedroom where he threw all the crack rocks he had on the bed. We started smoking. He smoked his stuff; I smoked mine. After a while, I was ready to go, but the man had a different idea.

"I want you to be one of my girls," he said. I knew what he meant; he wanted to be my pimp. I was too frightened to respond. I knew this was a dangerous man. I knew he was dangerous when I saw him on the street and followed him to the house, but my need to get away from the cops overrode my common sense, and now I was stuck.

"You are going to make me money," he said in an angry, demanding tone.

I just looked at the man, still not saying a word. He knew I didn't like his proposal. It was the first time I was really scared while living on the streets. I just looked at the man. He started cussing and screaming at me. He barred the door, locking me in the bedroom. I stayed in that room alone for three days.

I knew when it was day and night because of the type of light shining through the boarded windows. There was a heavy rain outside and tropical storm weather. At least I wasn't out in the elements. I felt my way around the room and found a door that led to a bathroom. I slept most of the three days, coming down off the crack high that had started the nightmare I was now living.

On the fourth day, the man came in, grabbed my arm and said, "It's time for you to go to work."

"There is no way I can make money in this rain," I complained.

He dragged me out to the street anyway, shoving me into the front seat of a car parked near a curb. He was angry with me and slammed my head against the windshield. He was cussing me out, calling me all kinds of vulgar names. He was trying to make me afraid of him, so I would do whatever he said to do.

He drove down the street until we reached an intersection. The car stopped, and the man pushed me out. "Stand on the corner!" He barked.

I stood on the street corner, soaking wet. I looked awful. The car started to circle the block. When it came back to where I stood, the pimp stuck his head out of the window to give me more orders. "I'm sending a man to you. Go into that building with him," he nodded at an abandoned building behind where I stood. "I'll be waiting for you when you come back with the money," he said as the car began to pull away.

The client came, and I turned a trick with him inside of the building. I came out of the building and walked back into the storm. I didn't see the pimp or his car anywhere around. My immediate reaction was to run, and I did. I ran as fast as I could in the rain, crying hysterically. I was afraid the pimp would see me running, and I'd be as good as dead.

I finally reached a corner gas station. There was a man pumping gas. I ran right up to him. "I'll do anything you want if you will take me out of this neighborhood," I said as I cried. "Please, just get me out of here!"

"Do you need to go to the hospital?" He asked.

"No, sir. Please just get me out of here. I'll do anything."
I climbed into the man's car and hid in the floorboard of
the backseat.

When he finally finished pumping the gas, we drove
away. I cowered on the floor until we were completely out
of the neighborhood. We drove to another part of the city,
and I began to feel safer. I told him it was okay to let me
out.

Unlike many men I had encountered in my recent life,
the driver didn't want anything from me. When I climbed
out of the car, all he said was, "Be safe, and take care of
yourself."

In every profession and every walk of life there are people who are real, and people who are fake. It's not so much measured by the work they do, but by their integrity and human dignity. I was a real prostitute, honest about who I was and what I was doing. I was also naive enough to think that every policeman was really doing his job, enforcing the laws of the land. One night I learned first hand just how messed up some cops patrolling the street really are. That's not to say that all cops are crooked. I just happened to encounter a few who were.

I was riding around with my friend Jessica that night. We had drugs in the car. When the blue lights started flashing behind us, I knew we were in for it. "We are about to go to jail!" I exclaimed.

She looked at me and said, "Don't say that. We aren't going to jail. Just give me a minute." She got out of the car and went over to the police officer. She spent about ten minutes with him in his car, came back and said, "Okay let's go."

I may have been naïve; however, it didn't take much for me to figure out what transpired in that official city vehicle with an officer of the law. That wasn't the last time I witnessed a cop use a prostitute. It happened again with Tonya, another prostitute, but this time it was a planned rendezvous. "A police officer is going to pick me up at one in the morning," Tonya told me. I didn't believe her; I wanted to go see for myself. I hid behind a building. I watched Tonya get into the police car. They drove around the block for about five minutes. When she got out of the car she had a handful of cash.

The Men

For the most part, there isn't much to say about the men that pick up prostitutes, whether they are cops or not. They pay money, they get a trick, and then they are gone. It isn't always like that. Sometimes the unexpected happens. Sometimes the prostitute ends up with a man who just wants to talk. The prostitute then becomes a very highly paid, uneducated and untrained, very unhelpful counselor. One man in particular stands out in my mind.

He was dressed in a nice suit, walking down the street in my neighborhood. There was no other reason for him to be there except for drugs, so I decided I'd go help him out. He looked like he had money. Maybe I could work for some of that cash. Besides that, the man was a red flag for cops, dressed that way in our part of town.

"Hey!" I said to the man. "You need to get off the streets 'cause if the cops come they will know you are here for cocaine or somethin'."

He looked at me, wide-eyed. "Where do I go?" He asked.

"Get behind that bush," I pointed to a large shrub between two houses. "I'll help you get what you want."

"I want some crack," he said as he handed me a wad of cash. I found a runner and placed the order.

"Why don't you come to my place? We'll get high," the man in the nice suit offered. He told me he lived in a one-bedroom condo on the beach. When he mentioned

56

the location, I knew it was very expensive beach front property.

We arrived at the high-rise on the beach. His place was fancy, a one bedroom with a balcony. The view overlooking the ocean was amazing.

"My family owns a restaurant," he said as we started smoking. He didn't offer any further details. "Hey..." The man began slowly. "There is something I need to talk about." He looked at me like I was the only safe person he could confide in. I nodded my head giving him the go ahead. "I've never told anyone about this," he said as he looked me in the eyes and started crying. He told me he was addicted to child porn.

Now, I had heard a lot of craziness from men that picked me up. Some married men hire a hooker and then regret it and end up sharing some sad tale about a wife who doesn't understand them, or that they've had some major argument with her over money or the kids. They pay the money with no strings attached. They want a listening ear, not a warm body. They just want someone they can talk to with nothing physical or emotional involved. They don't want a relationship; they just want someone to listen to them without judgment or manipulation.

That was how it was with this man. He didn't want to sleep with me. He wanted to confess his secret sin. He was caught up in something he could not escape. I must admit when he shared his secret, I wasn't quite sure how to react. I sat there, listening to him talk, while I smoked and got high. The man sat there crying. He was chained by an addiction he could not break. Guilt from his addiction drove him to numb his soul with crack and heroin.

It was terrible to hear about this man's addiction. All I could do was sit there and look at him. I had no words of advice to help him. I didn't really care to help him anyway; I just wanted the money that would buy my next high.

Not all of the men I met on the street were there for selfish reasons. There was one man who came to all of the crack hotels every Friday and Saturday night. He popped the trunk of his car, and passed out hundreds of free condoms. He would get the attention of all of the girls and they would come around and grab as much protection as they could carry. Then the man drove on to the next hotel. There is no telling how many lives that man saved, or how much disease he prevented. I don't know his name. I don't know his story. He didn't do drugs with us or hang out with us. He just showed up every weekend and did what he could to prevent the spread of disease and death among the street people of the city.

The Women

I said before I learned a lot on the street. One of the most important things I learned was that the women on the street deal with much deeper issues other than drug abuse and prostitution. Many of the women are scarred emotionally, physically and psychologically—often by the people closest to them. They live in a dark, unsafe and unloving world.

When the women were in their clean and sober states, they were very compassionate and kindhearted. For the most part, they had good intentions, wanted to do the right things in life, and didn't want to hurt anyone. Some dreamed of one day having a home, a husband and children of their own. Unfortunately, they were clean only for a few days before the drugs drew them back into the never-ending cycle of drug addiction and prostitution.

Compared to most stories I heard on the street, my childhood story was one of the best. I didn't go through half of what my friends did; they grew up constantly manipulated and abused. Most were from extremely dysfunctional homes. Before ever living on the street, they had already experienced psychological, physical and sexual abuse. Many also suffered from mental illnesses. My home life was not perfect, but my hardships did not compare to what others endured. The women listened to my story and said they wished their families were like mine. "You have a nice apartment. You have a nice used car. I wish I had that," some said.

Allow me to share a few stories about the women I met on the street. The stories go beyond drugs and prostitution to reveal the hearts and minds of the women. I couldn't help but have compassion for them, even in the midst of trauma and chaos.

Jessica was my best friend. She was in her thirties when I met her. She was like a mother to many of us girls. She always opened her home to us. She provided food, a safe place to sleep and a hot shower. Her home was like a haven; it was a place where we could rest for a few days and recover from whatever we faced on the streets. Jessica never took anything from us for staying in her home. She didn't make a dime from it. She had a strange kind of compassion toward prostituting women—maybe because she was doing it too.

Jessica's father molested her, not just once, but through her entire life. Jessica's father was a retired police officer. Anytime she got into trouble with the law her dad bailed her out. Theirs was a sick, twisted family. Her dad was her biggest enabler; he taught her she could make money from prostituting.

Another prostitute, Tonya, was schizophrenic. She ran away from her California home to escape her abusive, schizophrenic mother. She turned tricks with diesel truck drivers and traveled back and forth across the country. She liked Florida, so she decided to work the neighborhood instead of always staying on the road. I let her stay at my place for a few days.

One night, I heard her talking in the bathroom. It was crazy talk, a bunch of mumbling. I knocked on the bathroom door. "Are you okay?" I asked. She ignored me, but I kept knocking.

I heard glass shattering and when she finally opened the door, she had smashed a crack pipe on my white tile floor. She didn't just smash the pipe; she pounded the glass into the floor, over and over, with her bare hands. There was blood everywhere.

Seeing her surrounded by all that blood disgusted me. I rolled my eyes. "I don't even want to deal with this," I said under my breath. I let her wash her hands and get dressed, but then I immediately made her leave on foot. After she left, I cleaned up the blood with bleach. I never let her stay at my place again. Tonya was never in her right mind. She was never stable, whether drugs were in her system or not.

Gina was also severely mentally ill. She was known for going into hotel rooms, taking off all of her clothes and walking around. The strange thing about her was that everywhere Gina went she carried a Bible. I wonder what it was that drove her to keep the Bible so close at hand. Maybe she had an experience with God like I had at one point in my life, and clinging onto that Bible was her only hope.

Then there was Renee, another prostitute who was also addicted to drugs. She was a beautiful Latin with long, black curly hair. She looked like a supermodel when I met her. She had the potential to do anything in life and succeed, but for some reason she chose a life of drugs and prostitution. Renee was 18 or 19, very young for someone working the streets. She was the youngest of all of us, but I was next in line at age 21. Whenever there was a new girl on the streets, like Renee, all the men wanted her and were willing to pay. The men looked at new girls like they were fresh meat. It was completely degrading.

One day, the choices Renee made completely changed her life. She turned a trick without getting the money first. When she asked the man for the money, he pushed her out of his truck going fifty miles an hour down the highway. She was lying there, on the side of the road, all bloody. Thankfully, someone had compassion and stopped to help. They took her to a hospital.

When Jessica and I and several others went to pick Renee up from the hospital and bring her home, she wouldn't stop crying. The road burns on her body were so bad she couldn't wear clothes. We had to hold up sheets around her so she could walk out of the hospital without everyone seeing her bloodied, scraped up body.

Back at the house, Renee was in so much pain that all she wanted was to get high. I knew her cravings, and I felt sorry for her. I had some crack so I gave it to her to hold her off for a while, but it wasn't enough. Renee was so addicted that she couldn't even relax enough to recover. Even with us giving her drugs out of compassion for her pain, she had to have more.

She was upset because of her injuries. She sat on a chair, crying hysterically and said, "Who will buy me now? Who will want me after the way I look? Do you think I could still make money?" All she could think of was making money for drugs.

The afternoon she came home from the hospital, she wrapped a sheet around her body and walked out of the house in her bare feet. She was crying because she was so desperate for crack and heroine. "Renee, come back!" We called to her from the house. Renee looked so terrible that we knew no one was going to want to sleep with her. "Come back, you can't make money looking like that!" We yelled, but she didn't listen. She walked away from the house and never came back. She gave everything she had for her god—her cravings.

I never saw Renee again. She went missing, and there were all kinds of rumors on the street about what happened to her. Some said she went home to her family in the Carolinas. Others said that one of her dealers caught her stealing from him and killed her.

Thinking about what happened to Renee made me realize the power of addiction. I saw how addiction could turn a beautiful girl full of potential into a painful memory. I used to be a very judgmental person, but when

I saw these girls and their lives, and when I went through addiction myself, it made me less judgmental and more compassionate.

I realized that if I were to get hurt on the street I would have nowhere to go for help. I couldn't go to the police because my whole life was centered on drugs. I couldn't cry for help if I got raped because I was selling myself on the street to men I didn't know. I couldn't expect sympathy or help from anyone.

Not every woman stuck in the addiction and prostitution cycle was sold out to the street life. I sat and listened to a girl cry about how she didn't want to prostitute forever, but she didn't know how to get out of it. She didn't have hope. I wish I had known then what I know now. I wish I could go back and give her Jesus. He is the only hope for deliverance and recovery from drug addiction and prostitution.

6—ARRESTED

The first time I was arrested I was riding with Jessica in my station wagon. We had crack rocks in little bags spread across the dashboard of the car. The blue lights came on behind us out of nowhere. It was the police. Three cop cars surrounded my car and we stopped in front of a crack house.

Everyone in the crack house came out to watch. It was humiliating. My dealer stood there shaking his head at me as I cried. I was begging the cops not to take me to jail. They took me anyway. They made me sign a paper verifying what I was arrested for. I read the paper. It said, "possession of cocaine." I looked at the cop and shook my head. "I can't sign this. It's wrong. I can't go to jail for something I didn't do." I was determined not to go to jail unless the paper was accurate.

The cop gave me a questioning look. "I don't snort cocaine," I explained. "I don't do cocaine. I do crack." The cop shook his head. I had only smoked crack for a couple of months. I didn't know it was a form of cocaine.

"You should be ashamed of yourself," an officer said to Jessica. "This girl is just a kid, and you're getting her involved in this mess. She doesn't even know what drug she is doing." Jessica didn't respond.

They put us in the backseat. We were both handcuffed and on the way to the county jail. "Jessica, we are never going to see our families again," I whimpered. I thought I was going to jail forever.

"Is this your first time being arrested?" She asked in a tone of disbelief.

"Yes."

"You'll just get a little slap on the wrist. I'll see you in a few days after drug court. If you get to use your free phone call, call my dad and let him know what happened so he can get us out of jail." The only person I could call was Jessica's dad... the molester ex-cop.

We arrived at the jail where the cops processed my information and took my fingerprints. I had to pass through the men's side of the jail as I was escorted to the women's side. I was dressed to turn a trick. As I walked, the male inmates began screaming out at me: "Whore! Slut!" And other even more vulgar degrading names. I was so humiliated. I felt like trash and completely degraded. Verbally raped.

As a child, I never dreamed I would grow up to be a prostitute. That was not what I had planned for my life. That moment, walking down the corridor, is when I realized who I had become, and how people viewed me. There was no denying I was a prostitute, but that's not who I wanted to be.

How did I come to this in my life? It was my own choices that led me to my jail experience. I was the one out working the streets and corners, but it didn't all happen over night. One compromise after another led me down this path. As the power of my addiction grew over time, I found myself doing everything I said I would never do.

When I arrived at the women's holding cell, two female corrections officers brought me into a small, private room and instructed me to remove all my jewelry. They told me to take any barrettes, combs, hairpins or hair-bands out of my hair. Then they searched my hair to make sure I wasn't hiding anything in it. They told me to strip. I was made to bend over as far as I could and cough. The point of this was to see if I was smuggling any drugs in my body. If I had anything, it would fall out when I bent over and coughed.

They took all of my clothes, handed me an orange jumpsuit that was three times too big for me, and told me to get dressed. They led me to a holding cell full of women, all kinds of women.

Everyone looked a mess. Everything was a mess. The cell had one small, disgusting, stainless steel toilet in the middle. There was graffiti all over the walls. The cell smelled like feces and urine. It was freezing cold, and my nose started to run. There was no food, no water, and no toilet paper. We all had to go to the bathroom. We waited for the officers to bring us toilet paper; when they finally brought it, the women fought over it and how much each person could have.

After midnight, they handcuffed and shackled all of us together by twos, and loaded us onto a bus to go to prison for the night. When we arrived, they put us into another large room full of even more women. Another hour passed and they moved us again, this time into smaller cells. Early in the morning, they woke us up for breakfast and sent us to drug court.

At drug court, I sat in an area called "the box" where all inmates were required to sit. We waited for hours for them to call our names. I struggled to stay awake. If I missed my name, they wouldn't recall me that day. They finally called my name. Since it was my first arrest, the judge ordered me to attend a drug rehab, and let me go.

After completing a few months of rehab I went to live at a three-quarter-way house. A three-quarter-way house is a house for women who have completed rehab and are transitioning back into society to be productive, independent, clean and sober citizens. The house I lived at was in a very bad neighborhood. During the day, I was supposed to be job searching, but I didn't. I left each day, turned tricks and bought crack. Don't get me wrong, I had good intentions to begin with, but when I ran into a dealer on my way to fill out job applications, I was not strong enough to resist temptation.

One day, I went to a gas station to buy the parts I needed to make a crack pipe. I walked four blocks behind the three-quarter-way house because I didn't want anyone to suspect I was using or turning tricks. I really didn't want to get kicked out of the house. Next, I walked down the street to buy crack. I planned to smoke it outside, or in the bathroom while everyone at the house was sleeping, but I decided to take a hit on the way home.

I was feening and jonesing really bad. I saw a giant bush up ahead. It was the perfect spot to hide behind to take a hit. I was high within seconds. I came out of the bush and looked around. There was a sports car slowly creeping down the street toward me. The two men in the front seat were nicely dressed. I thought they might be interested in picking me up, so I smiled and waved at them. They pulled over. I thought they wanted to turn a trick with me; I was wrong. When the men stepped out of the car, I knew they were cops.

"Do you smoke crack?" The interrogation began.

There was no point in me lying. "Yes, I do."

"When was the last time you used?"

"Oh, hours ago," I said, lying.

"Ma'am, do you know where you are?"

"I'm walking down the street."

"Ma'am, you just came out of a bush."

"Yeah, okay, yeah, I did," I admitted.

They turned me around and showed me that the bush I came out of was on the property of a church. "Do you have anything on you?" They asked.

"Yes."

"Where is it?"

"It's in my purse," I said as I handed it over. I started worrying about the cops burning their hands on the pipe in my purse, so I warned them. "Be careful, you might not want to stick your hand in that purse, you might burn yourself."

One of the cops looked at me and said, "And you haven't smoked in hours?"

"Yeah, that's right, I haven't smoked in hours."

The cop shook his head. "You remember me? I was one of the cops that arrested you the first time you were arrested. One time was not enough, huh? You need to go back to jail again?"

I didn't respond. After another few nights in jail, I went to drug court and the judge ordered me to attend another rehab. In all, I attended seven different rehab centers, some in-patient and some out-patient. I transitioned between the rehabs between arrests, and sometimes because of behavioral issues that resulted in suspension from a program.

One of the rehabs I was in had a side of the facility specifically dedicated for people with HIV and AIDS who also struggled with addictions. There was a patient there named Troy. He was very good-looking, muscular and athletic. All the girls loved him. Everyone knew he had HIV, but he had a great personality, was fun, and straight, so the girls wanted him despite the HIV.

There were many people with the virus where I lived in Florida, so the fact that a person was HIV positive didn't matter because the culture was open-minded. The mentality about HIV was different than in places where HIV isn't common. People were educated that it is possible to have intimate relationships, and even to have children, without spreading the virus; however, that required much care and constant attention to health and wellness.

A few weeks after I left the rehab where I met Troy, I relapsed. I walked into a crack house full of people using drugs. I entered a side room and a man called out to me, "Angel! Angel!" I didn't know who the man was. He wore nothing but a pair of boxer shorts. He looked terrible. He was skinny, boney and he had lesions all over his chest. His cheeks were sunken into his face.

"Angel, you don't remember me?" He asked.

I had no clue who he was.

"I'm Troy," he said.

I was shocked. He looked totally different from when I saw him only a few weeks before. Troy's body declined fast on drugs because of the HIV. It was horrible. I didn't know what to say.

Troy was upset because I didn't recognize him. The reality of his situation was depressing. He sat down on the floor and turned the radio on. A soulful, Christian song began to play. We all sat there smoking crack, listening to the song.

All of a sudden, Troy started crying. "What are we doing? What are we doing?" He asked. "Why can't we stop? I just can't stop. Angel, nobody loves me. Nobody wants to touch me. Nobody will kiss me. Everyone is scared of me. Why can't I stop smoking this stuff?"

Troy knew he was in the final stages of his life. He destroyed his body with drugs. The addiction was his real problem, not the virus. Because his immune system was so low, the effects of the crack were even worse than they would have been if he had not been HIV positive.

Troy walked out of the room, and a woman walked up to me. She didn't know Troy and I knew each other from rehab. She leaned over to me and said, "Don't mess with him, he's got the ninja," she warned. I found out that on the street, people called HIV "the ninja."

I walked out of that crack house so distraught over what I had seen and heard. The reality of Troy's life was ruining my high and wasting my money. I felt sorry for him. His situation was one of the most devastating I've ever seen. Despite HIV, Troy could have lived a full life span if only he had the power to recover from his addiction. His is just one story of many.

In between rehabs, I was arrested a third and last time. At this point, I was in a very bad place in my addiction. I was very addicted to crack. I didn't even enjoy the high anymore. I hated it all. It was not enjoyable. I had to prostitute in order to get crack and survive. My addictive lifestyle became a dreaded job.

The night I was arrested, I walked down a street known for prostitution and drugs. It was back in the day of pay phones, and there were pay phones and hotels everywhere. To get drugs, all anyone had to do was call a drug dealer from a pay phone, place an order, and wait at a hotel for delivery.

I walked down the street until a man picked me up. He paid for a hotel room, and I followed him into the room. I was very tired that night. I just wanted to get it all over with so that I could have a hit. I started to undress and the man stopped me.

"You don't have to do this," he said insistently. "I don't want to do this. You don't have to do this to yourself. You don't have to live your life like this," he said. He put a wad of cash on the bed, handed me the key to the hotel room and walked out. I never saw the man again.

I was very surprised at the man's actions. I was surprised he didn't want to sleep with me. I was surprised that he paid for the hotel room. It made me uncomfortable that a total stranger could see something good in me. He could see something in me that I couldn't see in myself. He could see someone better than who I had become. I knew the man cared, and that compassion was something I hadn't felt in a long time.

At that time in my life I didn't have the strength or desire to believe in myself like he believed in me. I didn't want to feel what I felt, the pain of what I had done to myself. I didn't want to believe there was hope to change my life. It was too much work to change.

Why did he waste his money? I thought. I couldn't make sense of him. There was a part of me that wanted to cry, but I didn't let myself. I hardened my mind and heart. I refused to let down my guard. I pocketed the money, my pipe and the key to the hotel room, and headed out to get crack and bring it back to smoke.

I went to a pay phone in a store parking lot across the street from the hotel to call a dealer and place my order. While I was on the phone, a cop car pulled up behind me. I immediately hung up the phone to protect myself. I didn't want the cops to know I was talking to a dealer.

"Who were you on the phone with?" The policemen yelled.

"Nobody," I said.

"What do you have on you?" He asked accusingly.

I handed him my crack pipe.

He got on his radio and called for backup, "I've got a crack whore to arrest. Come up here," he said. Three or four other cops drove up. The first cop handcuffed me to his steering wheel through the open driver's side window. He started driving slowly around the parking lot as I walked beside the car.

"Look what I've got here!" He announced on the car's loudspeaker as if he were selling peanuts at a baseball game. "Crack whore! Crack whore! I've got a crack whore here." Everyone in the vicinity could clearly hear the echo of his humiliating call.

I started crying.

"What is wrong?" One of the cops asked in a daunting tone.

"I'm hungry and thirsty," I said. "I haven't eaten in days."

One of the cops left and brought back a pizza. They ate it in front of me. They drank water in front of me. They kept me as long as they could, humiliating me. I started screaming at them.

"Get in the back seat!" One of the cops ordered.

I began cussing at him.

"Cooperate, or I'll use the mace," he said.

I fought them as they tried to force me into the back seat of the police car. Finally they all picked me up and put me into the car.

"Oh, God!" I cried out from the backseat. I was angry, scared and upset all at the same time. I never felt so angry in my life. The cops' laughter, verbal abuse and threats made me feel worse about myself than I already felt.

"That's who you need to be calling on," a cop said from the front seat, "cause you're fixing to go to jail and only God can help you now."

Even though at that time I was angry at the cops, later in life I became grateful that they helped push me to the rock bottom in my addiction. Some of us in recovery from addiction refer to them as "the blue lights from Heaven."

When they took me into the jail that night, I had open sores all over my body from smoking crack and picking at my skin. I was malnourished and in such a mess, the guards didn't want me in a cell with the other women. They put me in a tiny cell by myself, not because I was dangerous, but because I looked sickly.

Once they transferred me to prison for the night, I was again placed in a cell by myself. The cell was the size of a small walk-in closet. A small bed with a thin mattress and a plastic pillow occupied one wall, and a tiny metal sink and toilet lined the other wall. It was freezing in the cell. There was a regular metal door with a small slot in it for passing food to me. Above the slot there was a square with small holes that I could look through. The holes allowed me to listen to what was going on outside of my cell.

I was in that cell for a few days. The night before my court date a female minister came and led a church service right outside of my cell. I could hear everything. The woman preached. The group sang songs. It was like a little piece of heaven. I don't remember what was said or what songs were sung, but I do remember the feelings I had listening. My life was full of darkness, but in my spirit I could feel a light piercing my soul. I prayed in that cell, and God met me there.

I was released the next day and told to return for my official court date in a few weeks. I signed a promissory note saying I would show up to court as requested. I left and went to Jessica's house. I decided to spend my last few weeks of freedom partying and getting high.

Finally my court date came, and I once again stood in front of the judge. I was awake for five days straight and I was drained and tired. I was eighty-nine pounds and twenty-three years old.

My mom was at the courthouse and seeing her made me angry because I wanted to use drugs and didn't want my mom trying to stop me. I didn't want Mom to see me the way I was that day. I didn't want her help. I didn't want anyone's help.

I had no desire to be free and clean from drugs. I wanted to stay on the street, or go to jail. I was sick of rehab. I didn't care to get help or to change. I had lost hope in myself, and had accepted the fact that I would never change.

"I want to do my time in jail. I don't want to waste any more of the state's money on rehab," I said to the judge. He was angry with me for so belligerently not caring about myself and my future.

"Look at the people in the box," he said pointing to the other prisoners at court that day. "These people have a rap sheet. They've been doing this longer than you've been alive. You haven't been on the street as long as some of them. You still have a chance.

"I've received several letters from your family members asking me to send you to Louisiana," he said. "I've decided to send you there, but I'm going to send you on an eighteen month administrative probation. And, I am going to require you to complete an in-patient rehab in the state of Louisiana."

AN UNDESERVED CHANCE

PART 2

After each arrest, I was ordered to go through a rehabilitation program. Rehab didn't work for me, mainly because I didn't let it. I relapsed as soon as I graduated each program. Before my last arrest in Florida when the judge agreed to send me to Louisiana, I had been in and out of six different rehab programs—some inpatient and some outpatient. Everywhere I went I was tested for diseases; each time I was released healthy, with no diagnosis.

It didn't matter how much progress I made at rehab, after graduation, I relapsed and found myself even more bound by my addictions. Here are some memories I have from my experiences surrounding rehab.

The Cottages

The Cottages was the first rehab I attended. It was near the ocean and set up like a little village with small stucco cottages scattered all over the campus. One section of The Cottages was for HIV positive people that were addicts. Another area was for addicts who were mothers with young children. Everyone at drug court wanted to go to The Cottages because it was more like a vacation resort than a rehab. The staff took us swimming at the beach.

We stayed busy at The Cottages. Each person met with a counselor regularly. Various groups met throughout each day: anger management, relapse prevention, and other focused programs. I will never forget my anger management teacher.

"Why do we have feelings?" She yelled one afternoon.

Were we supposed to answer the question? We sat silently looking at her.

"To feel them," she said calmly. "We were made with positive and negative feelings. As alcoholics and addicts, we don't know how to handle feelings that are uncomfortable to us and we mask our feelings by staying numb on drugs.

"As people in recovery, we must learn how to handle the emotions that we feel and be comfortable even with the negative feelings we have. It is okay to feel anger, sadness, rejection and hurt. God gave us all of our feelings to feel them."

I remember her lesson that day, but it didn't change me in a moment. No matter how great the teaching, counseling and mentoring, the problem was simply that I wasn't ready to change. Until I made up my mind for myself, nothing could persuade me, or force me to change.

The street lifestyle gave me a high as much as the crack did. I loved the spontaneity of not having a schedule, getting high whenever I wanted, making money quickly, and the freedom of not answering to anyone. After graduation, I left The Cottages and within three days was back on the streets using drugs.

New Directions

New Directions was a strict rehab program, more like a militant boot camp. The techs and counselors yelled in our faces. The idea was to break us down before trying to rebuild us.

One of the rules at New Directions was that we, the clients, were not to be in intimate relationships. The staff told us if we could keep a plant alive for one year, and then get a pet and keep the plant and animal alive for the second year, then we may be ready to have a healthy romantic relationship with a person.

The purpose for a time of singleness was to take time to focus on God and recovery and to learn to love and care for self—without the distraction of a relationship. It was about learning who you are and respecting yourself so you would know how to respect someone else. They took us plant shopping to begin our journey toward healthy relationships. I bought a small cactus.

The whole no-relationship rule was a joke for me. Even though I could have been sent to prison for breaking the rules, I had a rehab relationship. It wasn't much of a relationship; I really didn't care about the guy. I just enjoyed flirting with him. I had a stuffed animal that I sprayed with perfume and gave to my boyfriend as a present. A tech from the men's dorm found out about it and confronted me.

"ANGEL!" The tech yelled at me. "What is your teddy bear doing on a bed in the men's dorm?"

My eyes got really big. The tech looked at me, squinted his eyes, pursed his lips together, nodded his head, and said, "uh huh!"

He knew what was going on, and it scared me. I could go to jail for breaking the rules. Thankfully, he didn't report me, and I started following the no relationship rule. When I graduated New Directions, I went straight back to life on the street.

St. John's Rehab

St. John's was a very nice place. I met Dana there. We became friends almost immediately. We played spades and gin rummy together. Though it was against the rules, we gambled for cigarettes.

I completed St. John's Rehab and then relapsed again. One particular night, I mixed heroin and crack together. Out of my mind, I stood in the middle of a busy intersection. I was confused, and I couldn't figure out how to make it back to the sidewalk. I heard a voice calling to me.

"Angel! Get off the street. You're going to get killed!" It was Dana. She relapsed and was back on the streets too. She crossed the street in front of the traffic and grabbed my hand, dragging me back to the sidewalk.

Dana and I started hanging out after she saved me from the traffic. Overall, she wasn't as strung out on drugs as I was. She always tried to convince me to take care of myself. Once she locked me in a hotel room for three days to detox. She forced me to eat and sleep when all I wanted was drugs.

Dana and I started turning tricks together in order to make more money. She knew I wasn't using protection all of the time even though I knew the health risks. One day she got in my face and screamed, "You're going to die on these streets! You're going to die of AIDS on these streets because you don't protect yourself!" I never forgot what she said.

Dana and I were very close, but eventually my crack addiction ruined our friendship. When I had a choice between being in a room full of men smoking crack or hanging with my friend, I chose the crack every time. I realized my addiction was at a new level when crack meant more to me than my best friend.

One day, Dana was in a crisis and needed my support, but I stood her up to go smoke crack. After that, Dana was through with me. We stood in Jessica's kitchen as she cussed me out and threw crack rocks in my face. "This is all you care about anymore. You only care about crack!" She said.

I stood there crying. I knew what she said was true. I felt sorry about what she said, but not sorry enough to change. We never spoke again after that. I lost one of my closest friends because of my addiction.

The Choice House

The Choice House was a place for people dually diagnosed with addiction and at least one other emotional problem. It was mainly a psychiatric facility. I lived in a regular house, and shared a room with a girl younger than me. I had the freedom to come and go as I pleased.

While at The Choice House, the number one thing on my mind was making money. I decided to turn myself into more of a high-class prostitute than a crack whore. I fixed my nails and hair and started taking better care of myself. My plan was to turn tricks and stash the money instead of using it to buy drugs. I was just as addicted to the lifestyle of prostitution as I was to crack. It was harder for me to stop turning tricks than it was for me to stop using drugs. It was too easy to make money.

I walked into a different neighborhood, down a busy street, and flagged down random men. I came home each day and got an emotional high by pulling out all of my cash and throwing it all over the bed. I made hundreds in cash each night. I glorified the money.

In the middle of my insanity, there was a part of me that wanted God, and a part of me that wanted my life on the street. I could not make up my mind. Even though I knew I was actively living in sin, I tried to connect to God. Crystal bought me a Christian music CD for Christmas one year and I listened to it so often that I knew all the songs by heart. Depending on my mood, I played the CD as I looked at all of the money.

One day, I met a client who had heroin and crack in his car and I could not resist the temptation. I relapsed and came back to The Choice House after curfew. Of course, I was kicked out for my bad choices—they knew I had used.

New Way

At New Way each person lived in a separate tiny apartment that had one bedroom, a bathroom, a kitchenette, and a living area. While living there, I decided to enroll at a community college and begin a degree in psychology. I was finally following a program and doing well, until I met a crack dealer on the way to the bus stop. He gave me a hit, and then I turned a trick with him for more crack. I didn't make it to class that day.

I led a double life at that time. According to the rehab records, I was in college and doing great. What they didn't know was that at night, I was smoking crack and prostituting. There was a stucco wall between the New Way property and the rest of the neighborhood. I jumped the wall every night to get to the crack house. Eventually, I stopped going to class entirely. The people at the rehab still thought I was going to class; however, I was out on the streets fully addicted again.

One day, I met a man who looked like a football player. He promised to give me all the dope I wanted if I spent the day with him. We went to his mother's house and smoked. "Let's get out of here and go somewhere we can really get high," he said. "I have some money. I'm going to call a cab."

The taxi came, and the man I was with climbed into the front seat. I sat in the back seat alone. It seemed a little strange that he sat in the front seat with the driver, but I figured he sat up front to give the man directions.

We drove into a rough looking neighborhood, and the next thing I knew, the guy I was with grabbed the steering wheel and crashed the taxi into the front yard of a nearby house. He got out, pulled the taxi driver out of the car and started punching him, then grabbed the driver's cash from his pocket. I couldn't believe what was happening! As the punches flew, I heard a sickening thud and saw the taxi driver's teeth fly out of his mouth.

I started screaming, "What are you doing? You told me you had money!"

He screamed back, "Run as fast as you can! Go three blocks down and meet me at the house on the right."

I found the crack house and told the people inside about the man who sent me, and they let me in. The house was full of dealers and prostitutes. They led me to a bedroom where I waited for the man to arrive.

I was angry when he finally came through the door. As he walked in, I started telling him off. "What do you think you were doing?" I snapped.

The man held out his hands; they were full of crack. I had never seen that much crack at one time. We started smoking.

Ten minutes later, a SWAT team surrounded the house. The man I was with started moving furniture to block the bedroom door and window, as if he was going keep to keep the SWAT team out. I looked at him and said, "It's over. We're going down. We're busted. We have to surrender."

He shook his head as he lit his crack pipe again. After a few minutes of the SWAT team banging on the doors and windows, the man conceded and finally started moving the furniture out of the way. I started grabbing crack and stuffing my clothes with all the rocks I could carry. If I was going down, I was going down loaded, and if I got away, I wanted as much crack as I could have on me.

The SWAT team swarmed in. They cuffed the man, and a detective pulled me to the side. "I'm not here to arrest you," he said. "I know this is a crack house. I'm not even here to arrest the people smoking or dealing crack in here. I know what you were doing. You were sleeping with the man that beat up the taxi driver, weren't you?"

As I've mentioned before, I had my own code of ethics I lived by even in the depths of my drug addiction. There were times when I knew it was the best and safest thing to tell the truth, instead of trying to save myself.

"Yes, sir," I said.

"You were also smoking crack with him, weren't you? You are under the influence now."

"Yes, sir, I am," I said.

"Well, how long have you known that man?"

"I just met him today."

"Okay. I am going to need a statement from you on what happened to the taxi driver," he said. "Just to let you know, we've been looking for the man that you've been hanging out with all day for a long time. He is wanted for murder."

The agent took me to the police station and questioned me about what happened to the taxi driver. I sat in the police station answering questions one by one, as calmly and truthfully as I could, all the while knowing I was loaded with crack rocks. If they frisked me, I was done, but they didn't search me.

After I finished with my statement, the detective asked me if he could drive me home. He wanted to bring me somewhere safe. I told him to take me back to New Way. Needless to say, I got kicked out of that rehab as well.

After my third arrest, the judge ordered me to go to the hospital since I was so malnourished. All I did was sleep, eat and detox. I crashed without the crack, but I didn't have a choice any more. I burned all my bridges in Florida—with friends, family, rehabs, psychiatrists, police officers and judges. God was my only hope and answer. I knew I had to include Him in my recovery if I ever wanted to succeed.

My aunt and uncle from Louisiana called me at my mom's house. They said they attended church and told me if I wanted to go with them after I moved, they would arrange to pick me up. I said yes. I was excited at the prospect of going to church again, of finally having hope. I knew God and the support of a church was my answer.

At the hospital, the doctors gave me an I.V. full of vitamins. They tested me for diseases, and I was cleared as healthy. After about a week in the hospital, my mom took me to a thrift store and I picked out three outfits: one for court, one for church and one that was casual.

When I walked into the courtroom, the judge said I looked like a different person. He approved me to complete an inpatient rehab program and serve eighteen months administrative probation in Louisiana. I was on the way to my new life!

Despite the good news, I had a range of emotions during my transition. I knew I would never see any of my old friends again. I was going to Central Louisiana, to a town where I knew no one except my family. I was lonely, and grieving the loss of my friends and lifestyle. I was depressed and angry with myself for ruining my chances in Florida.

The Plane Ride to Central Louisiana

The one small bag I carried to the airport held everything I owned. At one point in my life I had two jobs, an apartment, a car, a cell phone and home phone—I lost it all to drugs. Most of all, I lost my dignity and reputation. I didn't want to imagine what my family must have thought of me. Did they see me only as a drug addict, or a crack whore? Could I ever have an identity as a respectable woman?

I boarded the plane and sat next to a window. It wasn't long before the plane rushed down the runway and took off into the sky. The thrill of the plane and being up in the sky was magnificent to me. I felt close to God flying in the plane, as if I were in the sky flying with Him. The only prayers I prayed while addicted were prayers begging God to let the drugs give me a good high, to not let the police catch me, and to let His angels protect me as I worked the streets. On the plane, I prayed my first repentant prayer since I was a child. I prayed silently, with all of my mind and all of my heart.

I talked to God like I would have talked to someone on the street. I didn't know exactly how to communicate with Him. "I like the way I live," I explained as I prayed. "I love the highs. I love the lifestyle. I like to party. I love the spontaneity of it all. But I know You don't like the way I live. If You can help me stop smoking crack, and if You can change the desires in my heart, so I will love what You love and hate what You hate, I promise I will change my life and sing in the church choir where I received the Holy Ghost."

When I finished my prayer, something in me changed. It was instantaneous. I knew the door to my past slammed shut, and would never open again. My life in Louisiana was going be totally different; it would be for the glory of God.

At twenty-three years old, in September of 2002, I stepped off of the plane and walked into a small Louisiana airport. I was to live at Dad and Crystal's house. I didn't stay there long, only for about a month. During that month, my aunt and uncle gave me a ride to the church I attended as a child.

At my very first church service, I walked down to the front, and a minister I met as a child came up to me and spoke a word from the Lord. What he said gave me hope through all of my recovery and still inspires me now.

"Angel, what have you done to yourself?" He asked. "You have been involved in great wickedness." He started shaking his head. "But the Lord has brought you to this city and this church because He has something for you to do here."

After the service, I walked up to one of the pastors and tapped him on the shoulder. He turned around and practically jumped; he was surprised to see me. I told him I moved back to Louisiana, that I had been messed up on crack and that I wanted to start going to church again. I talked so fast, I don't know if he heard everything I said.

As I talked, he reached inside his coat jacket and pulled out a small bottle of anointing oil. "Don't stop talking," he said, "but I'm going to pray for you and anoint you with oil right now!" He put a little bit of oil on his finger and placed it on my forehead, "In Jesus' Name!" He said in faith, agreeing with what I said about my life changing. He told me to call the church office and make an appointment to meet with him so he could find out how the church could help me spiritually. I called him the next day.

Two weeks later as I sat in the pastor's office, I felt the need to confess every wrong deed I ever committed. As I talked, the pastor's facial expressions showed his discomfort. He pulled his head back to the side as his eyes popped out a bit, and he clenched his teeth. It was as if he could feel the evil spirits that were attached to what I was saying. At certain points, he waved his hand at me and kindly interjected, "Let's not use those words." At the end of the appointment, I looked at him and asked, "So what do you think I should do about all this?"

"Well, Angel, all I'm gonna say is, you spend as much time as you want in the prayer room! And oh, Angel," he added, "the women's prayer room!" I smiled and stood up to walk out. He called out to me as I was leaving, "And I'm going to pray that God will put some strong, godly women in your path to mentor you."

A few weeks after that meeting, I prayed another prayer of repentance and apologized to God for my wrongs. I promised to change my ways and to start living right. From what I knew about God from childhood, I knew I had to pray for forgiveness and to repent of my sins. I didn't know what I was supposed to repent of other than drugs, fornication, and cussing. In my mind, all of my sins were based on my behaviors. I didn't understand the whole weight of what I needed forgiveness from—unseen sins like pride, jealousy, gossip, lying, and idolatry. All I knew was that I needed to make a serious commitment to God. I decided to be re-baptized to start with.

I felt so dirty. I was involved in so much evil, so much sexual sin, darkness and wickedness. I wanted to be re-baptized to clear my conscience. As I changed into a baptismal robe, I repented. "Jesus, please forgive me. I'm sorry for everything I have done. I want to start my life over and do it right this time."

I climbed into the baptismal tank and sat in the water as a preacher talked to me about the power of the Name of Jesus, and how being baptized in Jesus' Name washes all of our sins away. He told me to hold my nose and close my eyes, as he lowered me into the water. "Upon the confession of your faith, and in obedience to the Word of God, I now baptize you for the remission of your sins in the Name of Jesus Christ!"

I chose to be baptized out of obedience to Acts 2:38. I didn't have a supernatural experience as I thought I might, but it didn't matter that I didn't feel something special. I knew I was in God's will. People around me were congratulating me on my baptism, but I didn't know how to communicate with respectable people. I still held the street mentality "trust no one," and I was full of anger; however, I was determined to change.

At that time I didn't realize what it would take to give my life back to God. I thought all I had to do was pray and read my Bible, go to church and eventually start singing in the choir. I didn't understand the Bible. As a child, I attended a Christian school that emphasized The Beatitudes, so I decided to start reading the Bible there. I turned to Matthew 5:3-12. I read that passage of scripture over and over again. I also read the Ten Commandments, which are found in Exodus 20:2-17.

I didn't understand the emotional and mental change I would go through in becoming a Christian. When I first came back to church, I still had emotional walls up protecting my heart. I couldn't even relax enough to feel the love of God. Part of the reason I struggled so much to trust church people was because I was afraid I would trust the wrong person and end up hurt. Despite my feelings, I knew in my heart if I kept going to church and kept reaching out to God, eventually, I would learn to trust again.

I didn't trust anyone else, but I did trust God. I knew if I did my part He would not fail me. I did the right thing and kept going to church, even though the restoration process was slow. I didn't beg God to change me instantly. I wasn't in a rush; I knew it would take time. My faith was strong, even though my emotions didn't match. It was my mind that was determined.

I took responsibility for my previous choices, and I decided to change my life without the help of my family. I didn't feel it was fair for me to live with them after I had lived independently for so long. I felt I was disrupting their lives, even though they wanted me to stay with them. For my own self-respect, I had to make the right choices on my own.

I was staying clean while living with my family, but I didn't think I'd fully recover unless I continued to make the right choices independently. To get out on my own, I decided to move to a homeless shelter. My dad and Crystal were angry when I shared my decision with them.

"You are not homeless," they said. "So why are you going there?" I knew they wanted me home with them, but I knew I needed to focus, with no distractions, as I started this new journey of life.

The Homeless Shelter in Central Louisiana

I moved out almost right away. The homeless shelter I found had a program for people who struggled with addiction. They took us to recovery support groups regularly. I found a sponsor to help me work through the steps I needed to make in the recovery process. I also went to counseling. I always made sure to keep God first in my journey of recovery.

While at the shelter, I made several friends. We sat around chatting and smoking cigarettes. I had a guy friend in the group who was in recovery from heroin addiction. His name was Scott. One day, an outreach worker came from a local HIV/AIDS outreach organization to offer an HIV test to everyone at the center. Scott was on edge about the HIV test since he had used so many dirty needles with his habit.

Everyone except me participated in the HIV test. I refused to take the test because I was tested for HIV at the hospital in Florida before I moved. "I don't need that test," I said. I had not slept with anyone or done any drugs since my last test. There was no way I could have HIV.

Before the results came back, Scott whined about how he might have HIV. I constantly consoled him. "Even if you do have it, it's not a big deal," I said. "I know a lot of people who have HIV and they make it." As it turned out, Scott did not have HIV. He was fine. In fact, everyone's results came back clean.

Soon after that, I began to experience physical problems which demanded medical attention. For instance, I had a sty on my eye that was swollen for a week. I frequently had boils that had to be lanced, and I had staph infections. The doctors said my street lifestyle was so unsanitary that my skin would continue to detoxify from all of the drugs for quite some time.

While living at the homeless shelter, I had to follow all of the rules. I was only allowed to go to church once a week. I wanted to go more often, but I didn't have a choice. I had to work within the rules, so I called the church and asked for a van to come pick me up for services on Sunday night. I persuaded other people living in the shelter to come to church with me. We all rode the church van, and filled up an entire pew.

I lived at the homeless shelter for six months, and continued to attend church. During each worship service while the music played, the Lord whispered to my heart. It wasn't an audible voice, just His silent speaking to the innermost part of me. Every Sunday night He consistently spoke to my spirit, *"Something is fixing to happen in your life, and it's going to change your life forever."*

I was afraid of what was going to happen. Knowing me, I would relapse and end up in prison—that would change my whole life. "I am going to relapse," I thought to myself. "Well, I am not going to let that happen!" I determined.

The homeless shelter had to close down their addiction recovery program due to a lack of funds. All of us in the program had to find a place to stay. I called my uncle who was an attorney to see if graduating the shelter rehab program was enough to fulfill the obligations of my Florida probation. He found out that because the program wasn't a state program, it wasn't acceptable. I was angry that Florida didn't accept the program.

"I wasted six months of my life, and for what?" I asked, frustrated. "This is what God must have meant." At one point in my addiction, the disappointment of having to enter another program would have been excuse enough for me to relapse. This time was different. I didn't relapse. Instead, I started a new program.

My Uncle arranged for me to go to a local treatment center, a thirty-day in-patient rehab. "Y'all are throwing me into a rehab for people who just got out of detox or jail, and I've been clean on my own for six months!" I said exasperated.

My pride had me convinced I was better than the people in the program I was going to because I was further along in my recovery than other clients. After all, I had gone to church once a week faithfully for six months, and I was about to audition for the church choir. It was as if my progress counted for nothing, and I was sent back to the beginning to start over. My plans had to come to a complete halt. Once I started the program, I couldn't leave for the whole month.

The program, like others I graduated from, began with a required blood and urinalysis test to screen for health issues.

"Have you had an HIV test?" The nurse asked me.

"Yes. I had one six months ago, and I've been clean, sober and abstinent since then," I said.

The nurse looked at me and nodded. "You might want to get a second test because sometimes it takes a while to show up if someone is infected," she said.

"Okay," I relented.

The nurse began to ask the typical questions. "How many people have you been with? Protected or unprotected? Did you use needles to shoot drugs?" On and on she went, down the list of questions. I answered all of the questions honestly to the best of my knowledge, and she then administered the HIV test, and told me the results would come back in two weeks.

Finally, I was escorted to the women's wing of the building. I was ready for the month to be over, and it was just starting. The rehab required me to attend all group meetings. I had to go to fulfill my obligation, but I didn't have to be happy about it. I had an angry attitude toward everyone.

At one of the first group meetings, all of the clients sat in chairs arranged in a circle. In the middle of the circle were two more chairs. The counselor sat in one of the middle chairs. She called on each of us, one at a time, for our turn in the "hot seat." It seemed her whole job was to tear us down, question us, humble us, and make us serious about the program.

"Angelena," the counselor called out. It was my turn for the hot seat. Since it was my seventh rehab, I was ready for her.

"Why are you here?" She said with a snap as she leaned over toward my face.

I leaned back toward her and said in a matching tone, "Because I need your signature to get through with this program and get back to my life."

"Get out of that chair, and go sit back in your seat," she said with frustration. She couldn't break me down.

In addition to my bad attitude during group meetings, I purposefully isolated myself from the other clients. I didn't speak to anyone, and I didn't make friends. I only talked when someone directly asked me a question. I sat by myself when I smoked. I frowned and gave a distant reply to people who tried to befriend me. I wasn't there to make friends; I was there to fulfill an obligation.

The only person I talked to, besides the nurses and doctors, was a technician named Ms. Kathy. She worked the evening shift, and I talked to her when I had trouble sleeping. Ms. Kathy was also in recovery. She was honest and down to earth. I knew she was legitimate and sincere, and that made me feel safe. I trusted her.

At last, the thirty days were almost over. My friend Ms. Kathy was at work the day before my discharge, April 1, 2003. "Um, the nurse needs to see you," Ms. Kathy said to me.

I didn't think much of it. I figured I needed to sign off to release my medical records since I was leaving the next day. I headed to the nurse's office. The nurse was an older woman with grey hair. As I walked into her office she looked at me and shook her head.

"I'm so sorry," she said quickly. "I'm so sorry. I'm just so sorry." She looked both sad and nervous. At last she said, "You might want to shut the door."

I shut the door. "What's going on?" I asked.

"You might want to sit down," she said.

I didn't want to sit down, so I just stood there and asked again, "What's going on?"

Slowly, she opened my file and said, "You're blood work came back, and you tested positive for both Hepatitis B and HIV."

The instant I heard her say "HIV," my heart began pounding in my chest. I remembered God's warning to me during the church services. I knew in my spirit that this was what God meant when He told me something was going to happen that would change my life. The next thought I had was that this was only a ploy of the devil to get me to relapse. I was determined not to use HIV as an excuse to get high. After all, in my mind, I wasn't going to live with HIV forever; I believed I'd be healed once the church people prayed for me.

I looked at her wide-eyed and said, "Well, I've been going to church, and the Bible says that if the elders of the church pray for the sick, they will recover. When I get out of here, I'm going straight to church. They will pray for me, and that will be the end of it."

The old nurse looked at me, and her jaw dropped at my response.

"So what do I need to do when I leave tomorrow?" I asked. "Do I need to see a special doctor or take medicine?"

The nurse regained her composure. "We will get all that ready for you," she said. "Is there anyone in your family you want to call?"

"My mom in South Florida," I said.

The nurse pointed to the phone, and I dialed the number. After a couple of rings, Mom answered.

"Hey Mom," I said lightheartedly. "I kind of have some bad news."

"What is it?" She snapped. Maybe she thought I had relapsed, even though I was seven months clean, I still had a history of relapse and disappointing my family.

"Well, all my blood tests came back," I said nonchalantly. "And?"

"I tested positive for HIV and Hepatitis B," I told her.

There was a pause on the other end of the line, then a string of questions. "How do you know that for sure?

What if it's a false test? Can you ask them to retest you? What if they mixed up the results with someone else's results?" She was talking fast and was in obvious denial. I was the one in the family that was never sick, even during allergy and flu season. Now, at 24 years old, I was HIV positive and had Hepatitis B.

"Mom, do you want to talk to the nurse yourself?" I asked.

"Yes, I do," she said.

The nurse took the phone and listened to my mom. Finally she started to explain, "If we get a positive test, we have to retest everything a second time to verify before we tell the patient. That's why it took the whole month, instead of two weeks, for the results to come back."

I waited as the nurse answered my mother's questions, "Yes ma'am. Yes ma'am. Yes." The nurse hung up the phone and looked at me. "Your mother told me to tell you she loves you very much, but she cannot talk to you right now. She said she would talk to you tomorrow." I knew Mom couldn't talk to me because she was so overcome with devastation by the news of my diagnosis.

Next I called my dad. Crystal answered the phone and told me Dad was at work.

"Hey, listen, I need to tell you something," I said.

"Angel, I'm on the other line right now. Can you call me back later?" She huffed.

"It's important. You might want to hang up the other line," I said.

"Fine," she said. The phone clicked and in a few seconds she was back on the phone with me. "What is it, Angel? What do you need this time?"

"Well, my blood tests came back, and I'm HIV positive," I said.

A crying scream of fear blasted in my ear. I'm sure the nurse could hear Crystal from across the room. She was instantly in panic mode and began crying and asking questions. "Are you sure? What about my kids? Is it possible that we could have caught it? What is going to happen to you? Can you live around people? Do you have to be isolated?" She kept the questions coming.

She didn't know how HIV was transmitted. She asked if HIV spread by drinking after me, or using the same toilet as me. She didn't know anything about the virus except that it was something horrible that resulted in the death of many people.

The nurse interrupted the conversation. "If you want your family to come up here for a private visit, you can." I relayed the invitation.

"We'll be up there tonight, baby," Crystal said.

I hung up the phone and walked out of the nurse's office. The staff let me go outside to smoke a cigarette even though I was supposed to head to another group meeting. Ms. Kathy came outside and sat down near me.

"They are saying I'm HIV positive," I said after taking a few puffs on my cigarette.

"So what are you going to do now?" She asked. "Are you going to go out and smoke crack again? Are you going to give up and throw your life away because you have HIV?"

I looked up at her and said, "Until now, I have never been able to stay clean and sober. I have never been off of crack for six months. Me staying drug free this long is a miracle. I've never come this far before; I can't go back. There's nothing for me in that life."

She looked at me, nodded, smiled and said. "I knew you were different. You're not like everybody else. You're going to make it. I believe in you."

Later that afternoon, I sat down with the nurse and made a list of all the people I could remember I had slept with or shared a crack pipe with in Florida. I listed all of the crack houses, the hotels, and anything I could think of that would help me get in touch with people that may have been exposed to the virus.

I called Jessica's house first. Jessica was in prison when I called, but some people I knew were living at her house. An old friend of mine, Sharon, answered the phone.

"Hey Sharon, this is Angel. I'm in Louisiana. I just tested positive for HIV, and I wanted to let y'all know so y'all could get tested. I know I'm not the only one in our group of friends with it."

"You have a lot of nerve to call up here and tell us that you have HIV!" Sharon said with sass in her voice. There was a long awkward moment of silence before she continued, "And I respect you for that," she said.

That night, Crystal and my brother and sister came to see me at the rehab. I handed them pamphlets on HIV that explained how the virus spreads. Crystal cried and said how sorry she was for me.

My dad was working that night at the fire station. I never directly told my dad that I had HIV. I found out later how crushed he was when he found out about my diagnosis. We didn't talk about it for years. I think it was because he loved me so much that it was difficult for him to accept. Over time we have come to talk about it. It is a very sensitive subject even though we have a strong relationship.

The next day brought another challenge. I was released from the program, and had to find a new place to live. The halfway house I was scheduled to go to wouldn't take me now that I was on medication. So instead of staying in Central Louisiana, I went to another part of the state, to a Christian homeless shelter that allowed people with HIV to live there.

While there, I made friends in the recovery program. My aunt and uncle sent me preaching tapes from the church. After I listened to them, I passed the tapes on to my friends. On Sundays, I attended a small nearby church. During the week, I continued going to my addiction recovery support group meetings and counseling. I also went to doctors appointments and to pharmacies to pick up my HIV medication.

I remember when the nurse handed me an HIV pill for the first time. "These HIV pills are very powerful. It is very important that you take them exactly as prescribed," she said. "They will make you sick for a few weeks before the medication gets into your system. You will have to take medication for the rest of your life, in order to slow down the virus from multiplying in your system."

I experienced many side effects due to the medication. My eyes looked glassy, like I was stoned, even though I wasn't. I had stomach issues, and as time went by, my body temperature dropped and I lost energy. It was summertime in Louisiana with temperatures in the high 90s and sometimes above 100 degrees, yet I had the air conditioner turned off in my room, and was bundled up in a sweatshirt and sweatpants, freezing.

There was a lady living in the shelter that used to be a nurse. She noticed I wasn't getting up to eat, and that I wasn't socializing much. She came into my room and saw me shivering under the covers in my bed, even though the room felt like a sauna.

"Angel, there is something wrong with you. You've got to go to the hospital," she insisted. Not long after that, an ambulance came to pick me up. The doctors discovered that I was anemic, and I stayed at the hospital for a few days to receive blood transfusions. At the time, the doctors weren't sure if I was anemic naturally, or if the HIV medicine caused the anemia.

My dad and Crystal came to the hospital to see me. Dad in his funny way, wanted to make me feel better and smile. He left the hospital room and came back with a bag full of chocolate candy bars from a vending machine.

"You need to eat! You would feel better if you ate some chocolate," he said. His humor helped diminish the stress of the situation. None of us knew what life would be like for me with HIV. So far, the first round of medication wasn't easy. Thankfully, the blood transfusions gave me strength and energy again.

I stayed at the homeless shelter in South Louisiana for about six months before I returned to Central Louisiana where I rented my own apartment. My parents bought me a used car, and I started working at the mall. I was finally able to faithfully attend my church.

I still believed I would be healed from the virus as soon as the elders of the church prayed for me. James 5:14-15 reads, "Is any sick among you? Let him call for the elders of the church; and let them pray over him, anointing him with oil in the name of the Lord: And the prayer of faith shall save the sick, and the Lord shall raise him up; and if he have committed sins, they shall be forgiven him."

One Sunday night, I decided it was time for my healing. I wasn't afraid to ask them to pray for me. At that time, I was still a new Christian and I didn't realize the word "elders" in the verse did not necessarily mean elderly people. The word actually refers to mature Christians who are respected in the church for their wisdom and faith.

I walked into the church prayer room and found a group of old men. I tapped a man on the shoulder and said, "The doctors said I have HIV. I'm here to be prayed for because the Bible said if the elders of the church pray for the sick they shall recover."

The men looked a little shocked; however, I went ahead and raised my hands, bowed my head and waited for them to pray for me. They prayed, and I believed I was healed.

Again, as a new Christian, I didn't understand that the word "recover" referred to a process of healing over time. I thought it meant that an automatic instant miracle would occur.

Three weeks later I went to the doctor to find out my most recent lab results. On the way, I envisioned myself discovering I didn't have the virus. I planned to take my lab results to the church and share my testimony of complete healing. I expected a miracle. I was excited. I had no doubt in my mind or heart.

When I arrived at the doctor's office, the doctor said I was doing well on the meds. "You shouldn't worry about dying from HIV," she said. "When people are co-infected with HIV and Hepatitis B, the HIV destroys their immune system so it can not fight against the Hepatitis B. Eventually, your body will become so weak it will give in to the disease. You are doing fine with the HIV. You are very healthy considering your diagnosis." The doctor looked at me like I should be grateful. I was devastated and shocked that I still had HIV.

While I lived in Florida I met a man that was co-infected with both illnesses. He died peacefully of Hepatitis. If I had to choose, I would choose to die from Hepatitis rather than HIV. I watched people on the street die of HIV, and I saw how painful and destructive the virus was. I wanted it out of my system, but I was still infected with the virus.

I climbed into my car and drove to the prayer room at the church. I walked in crying hysterically. I felt wounded and as if God was playing with my mind. The thought of living as a Christian and having HIV went against everything I believed in. It didn't make sense to me that God would allow me to live with HIV. I thought that being a Christian meant that all my problems would go away. I didn't want to take responsibility or live with the consequences of my choices.

The pastor heard me crying from his office and found me in the prayer room. "Has anyone talked to you, or prayed with you?" He asked.

"No."

"What's going on?"

"I have HIV. I was prayed for and I believed I would be healed. I just went to the doctor, and it isn't gone!"

"I'm so sorry," he said. "Is there anything this church can do to make your life easier?"

I told him my heart's desire. "All I want is to be in the choir."

He began to smile. "Well, we would love to have you in the choir. In fact, I think it would be great for you to be involved in as many ministries as you want."

I nodded in agreement.

"Angel," he continued, "did you know we have an AIDS ministry at this church? If you come on Sunday, I will introduce you to Theresa, the lady who leads the AIDS ministry. Theresa is a good friend of mine. She is trustworthy. I want you to meet her."

I didn't understand why the pastor wanted me to meet Theresa. On Sunday, I skipped church because I didn't want to meet Theresa, and I didn't want to face the pastor. Later, I found out Theresa had a better understanding of my problems than the pastor did. I didn't think anyone could minister to me more effectively than he could, but he knew better.

I didn't stay away from church for too long. I really wanted to become involved; however, I knew I wasn't ready to join the choir because I wanted to quit smoking cigarettes first. I couldn't even last through a church service without leaving for a smoke. I knew smoking was harmful to my health, especially because of being HIV positive. If I wanted to live a full life span, I had to change my lifestyle, but I just wasn't able to break the habit.

I learned quickly that my physical choices directly impacted my spiritual wellbeing. The Bible called my body the temple of God, but I had damaged my body with my ungodly lifestyle. I still needed to work to transform my life. Everything had to change. I didn't have the power within myself to make the drastic changes—I needed God's help.

I wanted to be as healthy as possible and that required eating right and taking my medication, as well as breaking my smoking habit. Learning to eat nutritiously took time. Up to this point in my life, I ate donuts, sweets, fried foods, or fast food when I was hungry. I had to learn to like fruits and vegetables. That was the easy part. The challenge came when I had to depend on God to break my cigarette habit.

I decided to go on a fast and pray for deliverance from cigarette addiction. My fast lasted three days. I ate nothing and drank only water, but I continued to smoke. I prayed for a scripture to guide me to total freedom from addiction. I read Matthew 4:10 which tells what Jesus said in response to Satan's temptation. "Then saith Jesus unto him, Get thee hence, Satan: for it is written, Thou shalt worship the Lord thy God and Him only shalt thou serve."

As I prayed about this scripture, God showed me cigarettes were an idol in my life. My whole day revolved around smoking. I wanted Jesus at the center of my life instead of cigarettes. Every time I was tempted to smoke, I repeated Matthew 4:10 out loud, and prayed for God to deliver me. Not long after that, I developed bronchitis. My throat was raw from coughing, so I couldn't smoke even if I wanted to. The bronchitis lasted for weeks, and by the time I recovered I was free from cigarette addiction and finally ready to join the choir.

One night at choir practice, I saw a girl looking at me from across the room. "Hi! I'm Jenny," she called out. "Would you like to sit by me?" I ignored her, turned my head away and sat by someone else. At practice a week later, Jenny asked me to sit with her again. It took a few weeks of her asking, but I finally sat with her. I found out we lived in the same apartment complex. We started hanging out together and became friends.

Our friendship revolved around Christ. We watched preaching videos, traded inspirational books, and prayed together. Jenny loved God and was an inspiration to me. She exemplified the compassion of God. She had a heart for people and constantly reached out to help others. "I always pray about who my friends should be," she told me one day. "The Lord told me we would be friends."

One Thursday morning, Jenny convinced me to attend a Bible study taught by a lady minister. I stood in the back of the class, away from everyone. At the end of the study, I walked up to the teacher and whispered in her ear, "I'm HIV positive. Will you pray for God to heal me?"

The lady whispered back, "I am not afraid of you. I accept you, and I love you. Yes, of course, I will pray for you." She whispered her prayer in my ear so that no one could hear what she was saying. Afterward, she hugged me and said, "There is someone I want you to meet. She is a good friend of mine. Her name is Theresa." I looked at the lady, angrily. "What is it with these people wanting me to meet this Theresa?" I thought.

"Come find me Sunday morning, and I will introduce you to Theresa," the lady minister said. "She is trustworthy. You need to meet her." Her words were almost identical to the words the pastor used the day he found me crying in the prayer room, but I was still against meeting Theresa. I did not seek out the lady minister the next Sunday.

A few weeks later, I started to establish a schedule. I attended Bible study, choir rehearsals, addiction recovery meetings and church services. I did everything I could to learn from the people around me. I often imitated what I saw them do.

At one Sunday night church service, I decided to pray for my friend Jenny, even though she didn't ask me to pray for her. I felt it was okay to pray for her since we were good friends. I put my hand on her shoulder and began to pray aloud. All of a sudden, the lady minister who taught the Bible study a few weeks earlier interrupted me. "Angel, honey, I know that you are praying right now, but I need to introduce you to someone," she said.

"How rude! I'm trying to pray!" I thought. The look on my face showed everything I was thinking. I ignored the woman and continued praying for Jenny. The woman interrupted me again.

"I know that you are praying really hard right now, but I also know that I need to introduce you to someone."

I opened my eyes, and Jenny opened her eyes. I gave Jenny a questioning look. She nodded for me to go ahead.

I turned around and looked at the lady minister. I noticed another woman stood next to her.

"This is my friend," the minister said. "She is going to mentor you into your ministry." She took our hands, held them together and began to pray over us.

At that moment, I realized the woman must be Theresa, the one I was trying to avoid. I recognized her from choir. In choir, Jenny sat on one side of me and this woman sat on the other. I had not officially met her, and did not realize who she was. She handed me her business card and told me to call her if I needed anything.

At home that night, I was confused. I didn't know what the words "ministry" or "mentor" meant. I looked them up in the dictionary, but it still didn't make sense to me. I didn't contact Theresa after I met her. I was having the time of my life learning and growing in God without Theresa mentoring me.

I was constantly on the go. I didn't waste a moment. I didn't know how much longer I had to live, and I was determined to spend every minute of life helping other people. I didn't know how to slow down or relax. I stayed busy going to church, going to recovery meetings, singing in choir, and hanging out with Jenny. I also sponsored people through my recovery program and volunteered in the community.

Along with everything else, I also worked part-time. It felt good to be responsible and take care of myself with a respectable job, but I really struggled financially. It was hard to accept life living check by check. When I lived on the street I never needed a dime. I could turn a trick for money, and make as much in one night as I made in two weeks working at the mall. I worked a respectable job for clean money, but it was a huge financial sacrifice and took a long time to adjust.

I thought I was living life to the fullest, but in reality I neglected to take care of myself. In the midst of my busy life, I was in and out of the hospital with boils and staph infections. My body was still adjusting to life without street drugs, and to taking the HIV medication. Every once and a while I had to have another blood transfusion for anemia. I often ignored my symptoms until the last minute.

One night, I felt very weak and the thought echoed in my mind, "Go to the hospital, now!" I knew it was the Lord leading me. I drove to the ER.

"I'm feeling weak," I said to the in-take nurse. "I am HIV positive and on medication. I've had blood transfusions and staph infections in the past. I don't know what is wrong with me right now," I explained. They assigned me to my own room and a nurse met me there.

After she drew my blood, the nurse said, "Did you come by ambulance, or did someone bring you here?"

"I drove myself," I answered, puzzled at her question.

"That's not possible," she said. "You hardly have any blood in your system. You don't have the strength to drive a car."

"Well, ma'am, I did drive myself," I insisted.

"We will have to keep you for a few days. You need several units of blood." As the nurses began the I.V. line, I fell asleep.

A little while later, half-asleep, I saw three tall figures dressed in white standing next to my bed. I couldn't see the details of their faces, but I heard them talking about me.

"She's going to kill herself if she doesn't slow down and start taking better care of herself," one of the voices said.

I thought they were doctors, and I was angry that they were talking about me, instead of talking directly to me, but I didn't have enough energy to express my aggravation at their lack of bedside manner.

Later, when I was fully awake, I called a nurse to my room and asked, "Who's been in my room today? When were the doctors here?"

The nurse looked confused. "Ma'am, nobody's been in your room today," she said. "The doctors aren't here yet."

Looking back, I believe I saw a vision and the three people must have been angels. God opened my eyes to the spirit realm as a warning to slow down. Afterward, I prioritized my schedule and began to focus on self-care, but I still allowed myself to participate in the activities that were most important to me.

In December, I sang in the Christmas concert with the choir. I loved being involved! With all of my exciting church activities, I was able to make it through the holidays clean and sober. The church held auditions for the Easter program, and I was selected to be a part of it! My role was to be a Jewish lady in the crowd. The cast stayed at the church for hours practicing. I loved every minute of it.

I listened to choir music in my car in order to learn my part to sing. One night, I was driving in horrific weather. It rained all day and was still pouring down on my way home from work. As I drove, I had the music turned up as loud as it would go, and I sang as loud as I could. The last lyric I sang was, "He's King of Kings, and Lord of Lords! Forever He shall reign!"

The next thing I knew, I woke up trapped in my car. There was glass everywhere. My airbag was inflated. I started screaming for help. The police came to my window, "Ma'am, it's going to be okay. We are going to get you out of here!" I blacked out again from the trauma. I don't remember the police prying me from the car, or how I ended up in the ambulance on the way to the Emergency Room.

At the hospital, my family and friends surrounded my bed. I was confused. I looked up at my dad and asked, "What happened?"

"You were in a three-car accident at a major intersection. You're okay," he said.

I felt overwhelmed and started to cry. A nurse started to pick the shattered glass out of my hair. "What do I look like, Daddy? Is my face and body all cut up from the glass?"

"No. You're fine," he said. "There's just glass in your hair and in your clothes."

A man I didn't recognize walked into the room. He said he was the driver of the car that hit me and he begged for forgiveness. "It's okay," I said. Then I asked my dad when we could pick up my car.

"Baby, your car is totaled," he explained. "The only thing not damaged was the driver's seat."

A policeman came to my hospital room to talk to me about the accident. He told me the only part of the car that worked was the sound system. "The music was still on full blast when we arrived at the scene," the cops said. "It kept repeating one line over and over again: He's King of Kings, and Lord of Lords! Forever He shall reign!"

The police couldn't turn it off. Everyone at the scene of the wreck heard the music.

I was well enough to leave the hospital that night. I had a few scratches and bruises, but no broken bones or brain damage. I spent a few days at my Dad's house recovering. It was nice to spend some time with my family.

Once I returned to my apartment, I realized I didn't have a way to get to church anymore. Jenny didn't own a car and now we both needed a ride. The only phone number I had was on the business card Theresa gave me. I didn't want to have to ask for help, but I called anyway.

"Hello," a voice answered.

"Is this Theresa?" I asked.

"Yes," she replied.

"This is Angel. I had a really bad car accident a few days ago. My car is totaled. I don't have a way to and from church. Can you help me?"

"Sure," she said.

For the next six months, Theresa drove me to and from both church and work. In the process she became my mentor, and taught me much about living the Christian life.

LIFE LESSONS

PART 3

Theresa

spent time with me weekly. She talked to me, and gave me practical, daily advice about living for God. I remember riding in the car with her discussing the wonderful ways God was changing my life. Out of convenience because I did not have transportation I often stayed in the spare bedroom at Theresa's house. I spent most of my time watching preaching videos, listening to sermons on tape, or reading books Theresa recommended.

The first book she gave me to read was about intercessory prayer. I had no idea what the word "intercessory" meant, but I wanted to learn how to pray, so I read the book. Intercessory prayer means praying on someone else's behalf.

I volunteered to join the church's 24-hour prayer team. I prayed a specified three-hour shift once a month. I prayed, asking God to forgive me of my sins and to bless my family, but after the first fifteen minutes, I didn't know what else to say. I didn't know how to fill up one hour talking to God, much less three. I honestly didn't know how to pray, but I wanted to learn.

I wanted to know everything there was about prayer. In addition to the books Theresa shared with me I found other books on prayer and read them as well. The problem with many of the books I read was that they taught me basic principles about the power of prayer, but they did not teach me the most elementary steps of what to say. Finally, I learned what to say in prayer by listening to worship music. I listened to the music and sang the lyrics to God. As I sang the songs I felt God's presence and love. I also learned what to say in prayer by listening to people pray aloud in the church prayer room. My faith continued to grow the more I prayed.

Preparation for the Easter drama, which began before my wreck, continued on. We began each practice with prayer. Sometimes prayer lasted just a few minutes. Sometimes there was a divine outpouring of God's Spirit, and we spent more time praying than practicing. The Spirit of God was always strong at drama practice. It was an extraordinary experience to see people humbled by the power of God, kneeling and praying, and sometimes laying on the floor as they prayed in the Spirit. Everyone prayed for God to bless each performance, and minister to the audience.

There were children in the Easter drama too. One day, I walked into one of the Sunday school rooms and saw children praying and speaking in tongues. It reminded me of when I was their age. It was the same Sunday school classroom I prayed in when I was 10 and 11 years old. I sat on the floor with the children and prayed with them. I felt the Spirit of God moving in my soul, restoring me spiritually, and allowing me to re-experience childlike faith. I experienced a peace and joy in the Holy Ghost I hadn't felt in years. I was very happy.

The church used the Easter drama to draw people to Christ. Thousands of people from every denomination and religion, atheists and other non-religious people attended. The drama sold out every night for three weeks. My mom and step-dad from Florida flew in to see the drama.

"This is Broadway quality," Mom said after she saw the performance.

One night backstage, just before the production, my pastor's wife called me up in front of the cast and asked me to pray. "Say whatever the Lord wants you to say," she whispered in my ear. She then moved off of the platform, leaving me standing there speechless. Finally, the words came.

"Tonight may be the only opportunity some people in the audience have to experience the love of God," I said before I started praying. "Lord, I pray that our minds and hearts would be in unity and bring glory to You through this drama presentation."

That night, during one of the scenes of the production, I tripped and slid several feet across the front the church. The audience saw me fall. One of the actors, a disciple, helped me recover from my mishap. He reached down, pulled me up, and said, "Jesus is here!" I grabbed his hand and exited the stage as quickly as I could.

Despite my embarrassing clumsiness that night, God answered my prayer. The Spirit of God was strong in the sanctuary. The message of the cross of Christ and His resurrection was powerfully presented through live drama. Many people gave their lives to Christ. Many were filled with the Holy Ghost.

Afterward, I told Theresa how proud I was that the pastor's wife asked me to pray, and then how embarrassed I was when I tripped.

"Well, the Bible does say that pride goes before destruction, and a haughty spirit before a fall," she said, jokingly referring to Proverbs 16:18.

"I'm not ever going to do that scene again," I said. "No one will notice if one Jewish lady isn't there."

"You can't just quit because you made a mistake and fell down. It happens. People are human and humans make mistakes. You have to keep going," she said. "If you aren't in that scene, I'm going to tell the director that you skipped out."

I learned people become prideful when they forget how God changed their life. God had saved me from worse circumstances than this, I reminded myself. I decided to continue with the scene. What Theresa said made me think of something my mom always said to me.

"When you feel like you have it bad, just remember that someone else has it worse," Mom said. "And when you think you are 'all that' and you are better than great, remember there is someone better than you. Don't think too highly or too lowly of yourself, Angel."

One night after the production a man from the church came up to me and asked if I would come and talk to his kids, to share a part of my story with them. "Sure," I said. I couldn't wait to tell Theresa.

"Who is it that asked you to share your testimony?" She asked when I told her about the invitation.

"George," I said. "I guess he has three or four kids. He wants me to come to his house and talk to them."

"Angel, he doesn't want you to come talk to his kids at his house! That man is the pastor of the bus route kids! He has a hundred street kids in his ministry!"

"Oh!" I exclaimed. Once I found out how many people I'd be talking to, I was nervous. I decided to fast and pray about what to say. I decided to give my testimony and focus on Matthew 22:37: "Love the Lord your God with all of your heart, all your soul and all your might, and love your neighbor as yourself."

The day came for me to speak to them. I was shocked when a hundred children and teenagers walked into the room. Most were from poverty stricken neighborhoods. I was still nervous, but when I started speaking God took over and my nervousness went away.

I shared my story, but left out the part about my HIV diagnosis. The kids responded well. Many of them came to the altar and gave their lives to God. As I watched them respond to the love of God, I was thankful I had prepared myself through prayer and fasting. My obedience to God allowed His Spirit to flow through my story and bring hope to the group.

As my mentor, Theresa invited me to attend church services she was involved in at the women's prison. During the visits, a couple of ladies sang songs and various women shared their testimonies. Each service, I watched from the back of the room. No one ever asked me to do anything, even though I was faithful in my attendance to the prison ministry. I felt left out, but I didn't have the nerve to ask Theresa why I was there if no one was going to ask me to sing or testify. I felt sorry for myself as I watched everyone else participate.

I often felt devastated and worthless after leaving the prison services. I knew my attitude was not pleasing to God, but I couldn't help it. It was really how I felt. Finally, one night I went home and humbled myself before God. I kneeled down on the floor and cried out to God from my pain. The Lord heard my cry and spoke silently to my heart.

I see what is happening to you. I know you feel left out. I understand your pain. I am watching everything.

As the Holy Spirit comforted my heart, it felt as if God was right there holding me in His arms, telling me He empathized with my pain and validated my feelings. With that prayer, I laid down the heavy weight of my circumstance. From then on, I went to prison ministry with my mind on God instead of on myself.

Looking back, I understand why I wasn't asked to lead in the services. I had zeal, but I also had much to learn. I didn't understand what scriptures meant when I read the Bible. I didn't even know what the song lyrics meant when

I sang in the choir. Despite my lack of knowledge, I was in touch with the human experience of rejection and feeling like my leaders abandoned me.

Through disappointment, I learned how to be a better leader. I told God if He ever allowed me to lead a group, I promised to include everyone on the team. I promised to give everyone a job, even if it was a simple task. Later in my life, I had the opportunity to lead a prison service and I stayed true to my promise and included everyone.

A Spiritually Dry Season

There was a period of time when I went through a spiritually dry season where I felt nothing. When I first came to God, I was happy and full of energy, but during my dry season I lost my passion about living for God, and I was jealous of people who were enthusiastic about Christianity. I missed the excitement. I also began to question my faith.

"Do I really want to be a Christian?" I'd ask myself. I had many questions about the Bible. I started praying, and the Lord led me to the story of Adam and Eve in Genesis 3:1-5.

"Now the serpent was more subtil than any beast of the field which the Lord God had made. And he said unto the woman, 'Yea, hath God said, Ye shall not eat of every tree of the garden?'

"And the woman said unto the serpent, 'We may eat of the fruit of the trees of the garden: But of the fruit of the tree which is in the midst of the garden, God hath said, Ye shall not eat of it, neither shall ye touch it, lest ye die.'

"And the serpent said unto the woman, 'Ye shall not surely die: For God doth know that in the day ye eat thereof, then your eyes shall be opened, and ye shall be as gods, knowing good and evil.'"

As I read the scripture, God opened my mind to see the first thing that the devil did to deceive Eve was tempt her to question God's Word. I understood doubt was a tactic of the enemy of my soul. I was freed from concern over having doubts when I realized the presence of doubt did not mean I was filled with unbelief. Doubt and faith coexist when Satan shoots darts of doubt at my faith. I began to pray Mark 9:24, "Lord, I believe; help thou mine unbelief."

I learned to identify the mental attacks of the enemy and to fight back with the Word of God. Instead of surrendering to doubt, I began to find scriptures to combat the enemy and take authority over the thoughts of my mind.

Temptation

There were times when I experienced temptation through physical craving. God promised in the Bible that He would make a way of escape from temptation. The following verses helped me in those times.

1 Corinthians 10:13, "There hath no temptation taken you but such as is common to man: but God is faithful, who will not suffer you to be tempted above that ye are able; but will with the temptation also make a way of escape, that ye may be able to bear it."

James 4:7, "Submit yourselves therefore to God. Resist the devil, and he will flee from you."

The process of overcoming temptation was frustrating. Temptation in the form of drug craving often tormented me as I slept. I would dream I was using drugs even though I did not want to return to drugs, and I experienced the high in my dream.

In a psychology class I took, I learned that any change in life can bring a sense of loss, even if the loss is a good thing, like leaving the drug world. As my life and recovery progressed, I was, in a way, grieving the loss of the drugs, relationships and various aspects of my old life. I went through a process of letting go and moving forward.

I began to study rehab psychology, and I learned that drug dreams are a normal part of the rehabilitation process. I started sharing what I learned about drug dreams at recovery meetings.

"You're not going to use drugs even though you have a drug dream—unless you want to. A drug dream is how your brain asks what happened to the drugs and the highs. Your body is freaking out, but the truth is, you've already detoxed. Don't use a drug dream as your excuse to relapse.

"I don't have to act on every thought that goes through my head. Just because I have a thought about getting high, doesn't mean I have to go out and use. The truth is, I have all kind of thoughts, both good and bad, everyday. I can't control every thought, but I can control how long I dwell on each thought.

"I can learn to practice replacement thinking and make a conscious effort to make sure that every negative thought is replaced by an even stronger positive thought. When faced with temptation, I look for 'the way of escape' God promised me, and I replace tempting lies with a truth from the Word of God."

A Day to Overcome Disappointment

One particular day, I was overcome by my disappointment that God had not healed my body from disease. I felt angry, frustrated and confused, and I was sick of feeling that way. I decided to go for a walk toward the bayou near the church. I sat down in the grass and looked out over the water. I was determined I wasn't leaving that spot until I had an answer from God.

"Look at all the prayer, all the healing scriptures, all the fasting. I have prayed and believed for healing. I have lived my faith with everything within me," I vented to God.

The Lord silently spoke to my heart in His ever-understanding way. *And did you notice that I didn't do it? I didn't move in that area of your life, and you are angry about it. Don't you pray for My plan for your life?*

"Yes," I answered back in agreement.

Who's will are you living in when you get so angry? God asked me. *You are angry because I don't do what you want me to, but I do My will.*

I previously prayed for God to direct my life, but I became angry when I didn't like what happened. I had my own plans and my own idea of what God wanted for me, yet I convinced myself I had surrendered control over my life to Him. The real reason I was angry was because I really didn't want to accept His will. I wanted what I wanted. I wanted His plans for my life to match up with my plan. I demanded total healing, but God said no.

It was time to make a decision. Would I accept God's will for my life and live abundantly through it, or would I fight Him the whole way? I made the choice to let God direct my life. No, I was not perfectly okay with the fact that I wasn't going to have it all my way; however, I made peace in my heart with God's will.

I repented of trying to manipulate God and the spirit realm through my good works and prayers. I no longer lived my life to change God's will. I did not quit my faith, or give up on the grace extended to me just because life didn't go my way.

I left the bayou understanding more about God's will versus my own. I had a new realization of where my anger and frustration came from and what to do to change my feelings.

That day I placed my life in God's hands and in a moment everything changed. My worship changed. My prayers changed. I stopped asking God for what I wanted, and I started trusting Him with all areas of my life. I stopped spending my prayer time with just a list of petitions. I spent it praying for others, singing, rejoicing, and worshiping. I spent my prayer time surrendering to God's will and asking God to direct my life.

A friend told me they were mentoring a person who was having doubts about God. "If there is a God, why is there war and world hunger, abuse and disease? If there is a God, why do we have any of this?" The person asked my friend.

My friend responded, "That's none of your business. If God wants you to know, He will tell you." Her words stuck with me through each disappointment I experienced. I no longer lived my life trying to find all the answers. I found peace despite God saying no to my requests. I chose to live for God, and strove to obey the Bible.

The more

recovery meetings and church services I attended, the more I learned what I needed to change in my life. I felt convicted for the selfish and immature way I often still approached life, and I knew I had to repent. I felt regret over my past and what I had done to my body, my friends and my family. My confidence suffered because of guilt and shame. I had to learn the difference between conviction and condemnation. Conviction is an opportunity to see where I was wrong and to change the wrong to make it right. Condemnation is self-pity and criticizing myself over mistakes, instead of learning from my past.

I read a prophecy about Jesus' sacrifice for my sin in Isaiah 53:3-5. I learned Jesus chose to suffer to remove my guilt and shame.

"He is despised and rejected of men; a man of sorrows, and acquainted with grief: and we hid as it were our faces from him; he was despised and we esteemed him not. Surely he hath borne our griefs, and carried our sorrows: yet we did esteem him stricken, smitten of God and afflicted. But he was wounded for our transgressions, he was bruised for our iniquities: the chastisement of our peace was upon him; and with his stripes we are healed."

Despite knowing I could receive freedom from guilt and shame through Jesus, I had made so many bad decisions in the past that I no longer trusted my own decision-making skills. I decided I needed someone with a strong walk with God to make decisions for me, and Theresa seemed like the obvious person for me to rely on.

I saw Theresa as perfect, and I believed she could help me obtain perfection. I idolized her and expected her to help me make all of my decisions. I even asked her which of two jobs I should take. I couldn't make a decision without her approval.

In my past, when I didn't feel well emotionally, I used drugs to escape my feelings. Now, I had a new problem. When I was confused, overwhelmed, or dealing with negative emotions, I ran to Theresa to solve my problems, instead of running to God. My new drug of choice—I was addicted to people.

One day I talked to Theresa about my drug-using friends in Florida. The conversation was a turning point for me, and I learned something very important about life and relationships.

"There was just something different about Jessica," I said. "Our friendship wasn't totally right, but I don't know what exactly was wrong between us."

"She was older than you, wasn't she?" Theresa asked.

"Yes, she was like a mother to all of us girls on the street," I said. "I guess my whole life I have emotionally attached myself to an older woman, expecting her to fill a certain void in my life."

"You're looking for your own idea of what a mother should be," Theresa suggested.

She was right. I looked for the perfect mother figure for so many years, and each person I found couldn't live up to my unrealistic expectations. I ended up disappointed and miserable.

Theresa had an answer for me. "Stay right here," she said. "I'll be right back." She went to her bedroom for a few minutes and returned carrying a booklet. "Here, Angel, you need to read this." She handed it to me, and I read the title.

"Emotional Dependency. What does that mean?" I asked.

"Read it," she said. I read the booklet aloud to myself later that evening at my apartment.

"Emotional dependency occurs when one person depends on another person to meet all of their emotional needs. The emotionally dependent person believes they need the presence or nurturing of another person for emotional survival and security.

"An emotionally dependent relationship is made of two needy people. The strong person has the need to be needed. The other person, who appears weaker, controls the unhealthy relationship with manipulation. In reality, both people are using each other to meet an emotional need."

For the first time, I knew what my real issue was. I was weak and needed God, but instead I turned to people. Emotional dependency is a form of idolatry. I looked for a person, instead of God, to meet my emotional needs. "Wow," I said to myself. "I'm not the only one with this problem because there is a book about it! Many people must struggle with relationship challenges like I do!"

An idol is anything in my life that comes before my relationship with God. Over the years, I had idealized many people and material objects that became my idols. As a Christian, I had to remove all of my idols. Deuteronomy 6:4-5 is the scripture I found for this issue. It reads, "Hear, O Israel: The Lord our God is one Lord: And thou shalt love the Lord thy God with all thine heart, and with all thy soul, and with all thy might."

Leviticus 19:4 confirms God's thoughts on idolatry, "Turn ye not unto idols, nor make to yourselves molten gods: I am the Lord your God."

In time, God revealed to me who and what my idols were. As I confessed idolatry, I let go of all the people, ways, and attitudes that interfered with my relationship with God, and I turned to God with all of my heart, soul, mind and strength.

I felt relief in finally identifying this issue, but I was also embarrassed because I didn't have the ability to stop my emotional dependency. I realized emotional dependency was the biggest addiction of my life, and I had no idea how to begin recovery from the problem.

Knowing I had a problem with emotional dependency also made me angry. I had spent most of my life pursuing unhealthy relationships without having any idea that what I wanted was unhealthy. I felt cheated when I met someone with healthy social skills. I was jealous because I believed if I was taught emotional and social wellness as a child I may not have turned to drugs. Not only did I not know how to socialize, I also did not know how to be content alone.

Not long after Theresa gave me the emotional dependency booklet, she taught me about another concept that was new to me—boundaries.

"What are your boundaries?" Theresa asked me.

I didn't know what the question meant. My first thought was that boundaries were state lines and city limits. I had no idea that people and relationships had limits. I didn't understand healthy relationships had healthy boundaries.

"What do you mean, boundaries?" I asked.

"You know, where you draw the line and just won't take anymore from a person."

"What do you mean?" I had never enforced a boundary in my life, and I had no idea how to respect other people's boundaries. I constantly pushed to manipulate others to do what I wanted them to do. If I had a problem or needed something I called someone to help me, regardless of the time, day or night. Nothing was too bizarre to demand, whenever I wanted to demand it.

"I need to talk to you," Theresa said.

"Okay," I said with fearful anticipation. I felt as if Theresa was about to set a limit and a boundary with me.

"I'm not carrying you anymore," she said. "What God has for you isn't the same as what God has for me. God wants to take you to a place where I can't come with you. You have to be alone with God. You have to find your place and purpose with Him."

I sat there in silence, devastated.

"You are not welcome to come to my home as often as you have been coming," she said. "I will not answer your calls every time you call. I will answer only when I feel God wants me to answer the call. You can't depend on me for everything anymore. You need to be independent from me," she said.

My heart was broken by her words. I felt rejected. Theresa came into my life, mentored me, and now she was backing out, just like that? At that time, my world revolved around God and Theresa. I didn't understand why it had to change.

I started crying. "I prayed against people like you," I said through my tears. "I didn't want fake people or any hypocrites in my life. I wanted real Christians as my friends," I spat the words at her.

I was offended. I thought she didn't want to be my friend anymore. I could have easily given up on God, church, and staying clean at that moment, but I didn't. I was so angry and bitter. I didn't know how I could continue in my recovery and still go to the same church as Theresa. I didn't think I could face her at every service, choir practice and prayer meeting. I loved Theresa as my spiritual mother. How could I sit in the pew and watch her move on with her life, mentoring other people, while not having anything to do with me?

Theresa saw how upset I was and knew I needed time to process what happened. She let me stay at her house until I calmed down enough to drive to my apartment. I decided to make an appointment with my pastor to tell him how upset I was. To my astonishment, he saw things differently than I did.

"When you became clean and started going to church," he explained, "you were in such a messed up state you could not survive spiritually on your own. You were in spiritual ICU. God used Theresa as if she were your breathing machine. You were able to reach God through her for a while, but now you have recuperated, and you don't need a breathing machine any more. You can hear from God for yourself."

My counselor agreed with the pastor. "This is the root of why you have done everything that you have done wrong," she said. "When you get deliverance from emotional dependency, you will be emotionally healed and the person you were meant to be."

Everyone agreed, but I was powerless to overcome emotional dependency, so I turned to the Bible for help. I read the story of the children of Israel and how they wandered in circles in the wilderness for forty years with the same problems of doubt, unbelief, and complaining. When I read the story I thought, "These people are crazy! How could they not believe when they saw God do such miraculous things?"

But in reality I was just like them. God delivered me from crack cocaine and life on the street just as He delivered the Israelites from slavery in Egypt. Half of me was set free; however, the other half, the emotional half, was still wandering in my own wilderness.

At last, I accepted the truth. Theresa couldn't be who I wanted her to be. It wasn't God's will for her to make decisions for me. It wasn't His plan for me to put my trust in her; He wanted me to put my trust in Him. I pushed Theresa away by being too needy and putting expectations on her that she was never meant to fulfill.

My pastor's wife told me to completely detach myself from Theresa. "The answer to breaking free from emotional dependency is total detachment," she said. I didn't detach right away because I wasn't sure exactly how to detach.

After I left each church service I immediately called Theresa, trying to force the friendship into what it used to be. Afterward, I felt guilty and criticized myself for calling her. I felt like a hypocrite. As much as I wanted to submit to the Will of God, I continued to fail.

Despite the fact that I was still somewhat dependent on Theresa, I started gossiping about her to people at church. I felt she had wronged me. She hurt me, and I wanted people to know. I made it sound like Theresa abandoned me for no reason. It sounded much worse when I told the story than it was in actuality. Some of the people I gossiped to told me how wrong I was for talking about Theresa.

One lady explained it this way, "I don't talk about people because I know that I can make the same mistakes they have made. None of us are above failure."

Another person said, "How would you feel if you were the person who messed up and you overheard your friend talking about you the way you are talking about Theresa right now?"

I knew they were right and I shouldn't have gossiped. I found a verse to remind me how to behave. James 3:10-18 addresses the problem of gossip, slander and negativity. "Out of the same mouth proceedeth blessing and cursing. My brethren, these things ought not so to be. Doth a fountain send forth at the same place sweet water and bitter? Can the fig tree, my brethren, bear olive berries? Either a vine, figs? So can no fountain both yield salt water and fresh.

"Who is a wise man and endued with knowledge among you? Let him shew out of a good conversation his works with meekness of wisdom. But if ye have bitter envying and strife in your hearts, glory not, and lie not against the truth.

"This wisdom descendeth not from above, but is earthly, sensual, devilish. For where envying and strife is, there is confusion and every evil work. But the wisdom that is from above is first pure, then peaceable, gentle, and easy to be intreated, full of mercy and good fruits, without partiality, and without hypocrisy. And the fruit of righteousness is sown in peace of them that make peace."

After I allowed myself to process the pain of rejection, and I stopped gossiping, I finally began to believe that I was capable of living within boundaries, and that my life in Christ required a commitment to healthy limits. Now that I was aware of my problem with emotional dependency I wanted to guard myself from dependency and idolatry altogether, but I needed to start small. I couldn't expect myself to be perfect right away.

I began to set limits in every area of my life so that I could be healthy and balanced all the way around. I was independently starting to make the right choices. Setting boundaries when it came to substance abuse was easier for me than setting boundaries to guard from emotional dependency in relationships. As an addict in recovery, I knew I couldn't open the door for any kind of substance abuse in my life.

My family didn't know how to deal with the healthier me because I had never behaved in a healthy way before. I changed into a whole new person, and they had to get to know me all over again. While the rest of the family had New Year's Eve cheers, I abstained. My family didn't understand it when I first set limits with them, and said "no" when someone offered me an alcoholic drink at a family gathering. It didn't matter that they didn't understand. I established boundaries to protect myself from myself.

In the past, I went anywhere with anyone who showed me attention, regardless of their morals and values. It was time for me to begin to make new friends and operate within boundaries. I decided not go to clubs or bars to hang out with friends anymore.

A friend in her own recovery process gave me advice one day that made sense. She said, "If you hang out at the barber shop, you're eventually going to get your hair cut. If you hang out at the bars, eventually you're going to have a drink. It's going to happen if you put yourself in that environment. It doesn't matter if alcohol was not your original drug of choice. You are an addict. You can't control using any addictive substance."

Not only did I not want to be an addict again, I also did not want to become emotionally dependent on people who may lead me back to my old ways. I needed to make boundaries for myself to guard against relationships that could lead me back to addition.

It took years for me to overcome emotional dependency. I backed off slowly from people I felt drawn to, and I replaced the time I had previously spent in emotionally dependent relationships with time spent in ministry serving others. Over time, I learned how to set emotional limits and boundaries and was able to finally enjoy healthy relationships.

I began to pray for God to put the right people in my life. I didn't realize allowing new people in my life meant I had to make room for them by letting go of unhealthy friendships. Over time, I learned what healthy social boundaries were. Instead of feeling personally rejected when someone did not have time to be my close friend, I began to focus on and be thankful for the people in my life. At the same time, I began to struggle with the fear of rejection. I began sitting alone at church, isolating myself from everyone because of my fear.

One Sunday, a lady at church named Anastasia invited me to sit with her during service. "Are you going to continue to come to church and sit completely by yourself?" She asked in a foreign accent. "Come and sit with me."

The day I began sitting with Sister Anastasia in church she became a natural mentor in my life. I often went to her house for coffee and conversation. I vented to her about my life problems.

"Your life problems are your battle. You're going to have to fight it. It has nothing to do with anyone else, but you and God," she said.

Not long after that, I started reading a psychology book where I learned about projection. Any time I had a bad day, I took my problems out on everyone around me. I projected my feelings onto everyone else, but my feelings belonged to me and I had to learn to take responsibility for them.

In my recovery program, I learned that making amends was a requirement for healthy relationships. Feeling sorry and identifying my responsibility in relational conflicts was not enough. It was my job to make things right between me and everyone else. Making amends was not an easy thing to do, but it was important.

I remembered when my first step-dad, Cliff, made amends with me. He came back into my life when I was a teenager and said he was sorry for everything he did wrong during his active drug addiction when I was a child. I was using drugs during our conversation, and though I wasn't ready to begin my journey of recovery, hearing his story gave me hope that I could one day change. After that, my relationship with Cliff was restored. He always inspired me.

During my active addiction, my family and close friends often heard me say I was sorry for using drugs and for disappointing and disrespecting them. Every time I said I was sorry, I relapsed and hurt them again. My words didn't mean much to anyone anymore, so when it came time for me to restore my relationships, I had to show I had truly repented through my attitude and behavior.

At the start of my recovery journey, my relationship with my mother was restored. My mom and her husband Stanley were happy with the progress and changes I made in my lifestyle. I was finally clean and sober. I didn't have to prove anything to my mom. She was ready to move beyond the past.

Even though Dad and Crystal had divorced again, once I began making amends, I knew I needed to make things right with Crystal. I am thankful to say that Crystal and I settled our differences. It was a miraculous reconciliation! We forgave each other and became close. Occasionally, we studied the Bible together and sat together in church. Not long after we made amends, Crystal passed away unexpectedly. I am glad to know she made peace with God and with me before she died. I am grateful for her. I am also grateful for the wonderful woman Dad married before Crystal died who became a great part of our family.

I have learned that some of the people I have hurt are often not ready to receive my efforts toward restoration. If the other person is not ready to move forward in our relationship, I cannot allow that to control me. I have done my part, and I must let go of trying to force them to accept me. I give them time and space to heal from all of the damage I caused, regardless of how much time it takes each person. Just because I changed, doesn't mean everyone else in my life changed with me, or that they are ready to accept the changes I made.

My dad and I have always had a very close relationship. He affirmed me multiple times through my recovery. After years in recovery from addiction, my dad looked at me and said, "You are special. I knew that the moment you were born. Even with everything you've been through, you have a good life and are blessed.

"You are now the woman God has always wanted you to be. You don't have to live your life to prove anything anymore. We know that you've changed. We trust you." His words of confidence meant the world to me.

My grandmother also encouraged me. "You can do whatever you put your mind to," she said. "I'm proud of you and all the good things you are doing."

After making amends and hearing my family affirm me, I knew for sure it was possible to have a new identity, and to regain the respect of people I hurt. My life was transformed. I no longer lived for drugs or money. I became a woman of God, and my family recognized my new identity in Christ.

On the

plane ride to Louisiana from Florida, when I first made the decision to change my life, I thought I would miss the spontaneity of street life and partying. After years of recovery, I can confidently say I don't miss my old life and my life is still exciting and spontaneous. Even now, my mother and Stanley continue to take me with them on first-class trips around the world. We've been to Germany, France, Belgium, South Africa and England. I have greatly benefitted from my travels and am more culturally aware because of their investment in me.

At home in Louisiana, I started building healthy friendships. God led me to people in my age group that I could hang out and have fun with. I started learning how to relax and enjoy daily life. God blessed me with one particular friend named Holly.

"What do you want to look like on your wedding day?" Holly asked me one day. I didn't know what to say. The possibility of marriage had not crossed my mind. She answered for me. "You would want to look your very best. In the book of Revelations in the Bible, believers are called the bride of Christ. Just like a bride would want to look beautiful for her husband, we should do our best to look our best for God. When His people look respectable, God receives the glory."

Her advice made sense to me, and I started caring more about my appearance. I began fixing my hair and buying respectable clothing. Holly loved to shop, and I often went with her.

"I love shoes!" Holly said one day as we shopped.

"I like shoes, too!" I said. "I have almost twenty pairs of shoes." I thought owning twenty pairs of shoes was extreme.

"Twenty? Is that all? You need to come see my shoe collection." She invited me over to her house, and when she opened her closet, I was shocked. She had over one hundred pairs of shoes! She had to make special space for all of her shoes.

"Wow! And I thought I had a lot of shoes!" I said. "You know, there are recovery programs for people like you—addicted to shoe shopping!" We laughed at the irony of the situation.

Holly found out I wore the same size shoe as she did, and she started giving me some of her shoes. In the process, she found some shoes she didn't even remember buying. I still own the shoes she gave me.

Another day, Holly said, "I don't understand people who can only have one friend at a time. They don't know how to be friendly to everyone. It's like they try to have one person meet all of their emotional needs, instead of enjoying several friendships at the same time."

I didn't say anything to Holly about what she said concerning emotionally dependent people. I just listened. Holly had great boundaries. She taught me by example about the boundaries I needed in order to have close friendships. She set a great example of what it meant to be a true close friend.

Holly's parents were pastors. One day, I went out to eat with her family. I felt comfortable talking about my relationship with God with them. I told them that in the beginning of my conversion, everything seemed so exciting and happy, but now it seemed mundane.

"Your relationship with God is just like a marriage," Holly's mother told me. "When you first meet someone, you start flirting. You tell everyone about that person. It's fun and a little mysterious, even. Then you get married and you get to know that person. I may not have the goosebumps that I had when I first married, but now I know that man," she said pointing at her husband. "I know how he thinks. I know how he operates. I know what he is going to do before he does it.

"It's the same way with God. In the beginning, your relationship with God is new and exciting, but as you grow closer to Him, you begin to have the type of relationship that is close and caring. You know how God operates in your life, and you easily recognize His voice."

I am so thankful for the friendship I have with Jesus Christ and for all of the wonderful friends He has brought into my life. I wouldn't be where I am today if it were not for the many people like Theresa, Anastasia, Holly, other friends, and my family who showed me grace, mercy and love over the years.

It had been a couple of years since I stopped begging God to heal my physical body that day by the bayou. I belonged to God regardless of my physical status, diagnosis or daily medication regime. My faith in God's healing power remained even though I accepted that He may not heal me. I decided to live for Him no matter what.

Jesus bought my soul with the blood He shed on the cross. He became the sacrifice for my sin, and because He died for me, I can have eternal life. God offers me eternal life, but on earth my body still suffers the consequences of my choices.

I found scriptures that helped me accept my circumstances. 1 Corinthians 3:16-17 says, "Know ye not that ye are the temple of God, and that the Spirit of God dwelleth in you? If any man defile the temple of God, him shall God destroy; for the temple of God is Holy, which temple ye are." I defiled God's temple—my body—through sin, addiction and selfishness.

I wanted to worship God with my whole life, but old habits are hard to break. I still struggled with skin picking, but not to the extent that I had during my active addiction. I desperately wanted clear, pretty skin, but obsessive picking kept my skin scarred and scabbed. I wanted to stop, but Obsessive Compulsive Disorder was too powerful for me to overcome by myself.

One night I went to the church prayer room to pray, and God delivered me from OCD and picking at my skin. It was an immediate, supernatural healing. I haven't struggled with the problem since that night!

My mom wanted to know what happened. "Your skin is so clear and beautiful," she said. "How did you finally stop picking at it?"

"I didn't want to live that way anymore," I said. "One night I prayed and believed for God to deliver me from the habit. It was a miracle! God delivered me from the nervous thoughts that kept me trapped, searching and picking at imperfections. By His grace, I'll never obsessively pick at my skin again."

My deliverance from skin picking increased my faith in God as my Healer. I believed with all of my heart that God could heal me from anything. Each time I went to the doctor, I told myself, "I'll leave here with a clean bill of health."

My faith was challenged every time I went to the doctor and they confirmed that I still had HIV and Hepatitis B. I thought there must still be some sin in my life that kept me from receiving total healing. If my behavior led me to disease, changing my behavior could lead me to healing, I reasoned.

I tried everything: I witnessed, prayed and fasted. I believed I needed to prepare myself spiritually to accept a miracle. I kept trying to make myself into a better person. I was willing to do anything I needed to do to make myself worthy of healing. I did everything I could, and I still did not see results.

The problem was that all the "holy" behavior was a cover; I was still trying to manipulate God into giving me my will. On the outside, I was as good of a person as I could make myself, yet inside I was angry and bitter. I put myself through an internal hell, criticizing myself for my sickness—as if it were something I could control. With each lab result, I searched my mind and heart for what else I needed to change.

I thought it was God's will for me to marry, have children, and finish college. I could see myself working as a psychologist in rehab centers and professionally helping others overcome addiction, but those were my plans, not God's.

I experienced even more challenges when I began to attend college again. I had a hard time completing assignments. I couldn't comprehend or retain information the way others in my classes seemed to. I just couldn't stay focused.

Why was it so difficult for me? Was it because I was bipolar? Had I destroyed my brain with drug use? I was discouraged. My dream of working as psychologist wasn't working out the way I thought it should.

My sleeping patterns were also an issue. My mind would not shut down; it was as if there were a million thoughts racing through my brain all night long. I couldn't slow down my thoughts. I often stayed awake for two, or three days in a row, unless I took medication to help me sleep. After staying awake that long, I would crash for two, or three more days. I couldn't commit to work or school during morning hours, just in case I couldn't sleep the night before.

I experienced major high and low mood swings. After all, I had stopped taking my bipolar medication because I believed God healed me, and I didn't need the medication anymore. My highs were amazing. I loved the excitement of an emotional high. I was excited, happy and talkative. While I was on an emotional high, I gave my most effective testimonies while sharing in recovery groups because I felt more confidence.

My lows were as bad as my highs were good. I always came up with an excuse for my bad moods. I explained that I was experiencing a "spiritual attack" from the devil because of all of the good things I was doing. I was overly sensitive. I took everything everyone said very personally. I immediately looked for what was wrong in a situation and never focused on what was right.

My constant mood swings drove my friends crazy, and drove many of them away. As friends came and went, I questioned myself. Was I in the will of God? I was angry and frustrated with my life. No one seemed to understand me, or even try. I believed others judged me because I could not perform at standard levels.

One of my pastors sympathized, "It's easy for people to judge your situation when they are not living it. It's easy for them to have their own opinions on what you should do with your life. Of course, they have answers for you; they aren't experiencing what you are experiencing! Live your life for God. Don't worry about what they think of you; worry about what God thinks of you."

Along with my mood swings, I was out of balance in my faith in God. I read a book by a preacher who wrote about how he went through times questioning his faith. It eased my mind to know I wasn't the only one who wanted to believe in God, but still doubted.

I reached out to other believers for help. I e-mailed a preacher about my faith struggles. The preacher e-mailed me back. "Sometimes the greatest act of faith is to just keep the faith," he wrote.

I went back to the doctor because of all of my emotional symptoms. "You are decidedly Bipolar," the doctor told me. "You do all the typical things that Bipolar people do." I was offended at his words. I believed God healed me; however, the doctors said I was not healed, and I still needed medication. Here I was, a Christian—fasting, praying, helping others—and I still had to deal with Bipolar Disorder. It upset me that I had to take medication again.

I prayed for God to give me peace about taking the medication the doctors insisted I needed. I knew in my heart I still needed the medication, but I struggled with accepting the fact that I was Bipolar. I was afraid church people would label me weak or not spiritual if I took medication.

One day I was in the prayer room at the same time as my pastor's wife. I asked her what she thought about me taking medication for Bipolar Disorder.

"Angel," she said slowly, "Do you shave your arm pits, or does the Holy Ghost shave them for you?"

I didn't answer right away. Is this a trick question? I thought.

"Angel, you shave your arm pits. You do it. The Holy Ghost doesn't. There are some things the Holy Ghost is not going to do for you," she said. We laughed at what she said, but her analogy taught me that I must do my part, and trust that God will do His part.

Through this situation, God showed me that sometimes He uses doctors and medication to heal us. I had to accept that it was okay for God to answer prayers in other ways beyond supernatural, instantaneous healing. I decided to begin taking medication for Bipolar Disorder again.

I determined if half of my symptoms went away while on medication, I'd be happy and thank God for it. Even with medication, it would still be a miracle if I could sleep through the night. I gave God glory for providing doctors with knowledge to know how to help me.

The medication stabilized my mood swings and slowed my brain down so I could sleep. While on medicine, I was not as sensitive or as easily hurt emotionally. I was able to focus and experience a more normal life.

I still had concerns about my health. I often thought about dying and what death would be like. When I was first diagnosed as co-infected with HIV and Hepatitis B, the doctor told me I would one day die of Hepatitis, and I accepted that.

As I mentioned before, when I lived in Florida I witnessed someone die of Hepatitis B who was co-infected with HIV. It appeared he had a peaceful death. I was much more afraid of dying from AIDS.

People diagnosed with HIV, actually die from other infections they catch because their immune system is destroyed when the HIV progresses to AIDS. It's similar to when a person with cancer is more susceptible to infection because chemotherapy destroys their immune system. Medication for HIV slows down the virus from progressing to AIDS, but it doesn't make HIV totally go away.

Thankfully, I have not experienced many complications from HIV or Hepatitis B. God and my medication did its job. I am undetectable with HIV, meaning my t-cell count is high, and the amount of the virus in my viral load is low. I live life without any daily symptoms. Regardless of how well I seem, every year I must have annual tests completed to see if anything new shows up. I usually go to the doctor around Christmas and receive results in January.

In January 2011, I went to the doctor for my yearly results. It was a new doctor who only knew my current lab results, not my history. Hepatitis B affects liver enzymes, so I always asked about my enzyme levels because I was afraid of dying.

The doctor looked at the lab results. "There's nothing wrong with your liver," she said.

"Well, I have Hepatitis B. I like to know my levels," I explained.

"Your enzymes are in normal range," she said. "Your lab results are not showing you have Hepatitis B."

I was confused. "Look, I know I have it. Check my records. I was diagnosed years ago. I always check my liver enzymes when I have this check-up. What is going on?"

The doctor continued, "Evidently, Angelena, your immune system is so healthy, that even with HIV, it kicked out the Hepatitis B."

I was excited. I couldn't believe I didn't test positive for Hepatitis! When I left the doctor's office, I contacted my pastor's office and shared the good news.

My pastor was happy to hear what I had to say. "Can you get a copy of the medical form that says you were treated for Hepatitis B, and a copy of the new lab results?"

He asked. I made a copy of the results. The next Sunday, my pastor announced that I was healed for the glory of God!

I researched Hepatitis B. I learned that occasionally the virus does go away. It's funny because I hadn't even prayed very much for God to heal me from Hepatitis B. I always focused on the fact that I was HIV positive. It was a very unexpected healing.

Because Hepatitis B affects the liver, if a person smokes, drinks or does drugs, they die more quickly from the virus. I had a better chance of healing from Hepatitis B because I wasn't destroying my body through substance abuse. I always pray for God's favor as I take my medications, and that they will work in my body the way God wants them to. I am healthy today and living with HIV at undetectable levels because of God's hand on my life.

I met another person with Hepatitis B that asked me to pray for his healing. I prayed, and then I talked to him about it. "Are you still drinking or using drugs?" I asked. "Your faith is dead without works. You must pray and treat the substance abuse problem. As James Chapter 2 says, faith without works is dead! Place your trust in God, let Him make the ultimate decisions about your healing, and like me, you may just receive an unexpected miracle!"

Over the next several years, I progressed in my recovery, faithfully attended church, and matured in all areas of my life. I continued my involvement in prison ministry and eventually shared my full testimony and began teaching Bible studies.

I loved to teach Bible studies. Every Thursday, I invited some of the people I met at recovery meetings to come to my apartment where we ate dinner before I taught a lesson from the Bible. I learned more about the Bible as I prepared to teach each week.

Despite the evident growth in my life, I still had a problem with emotional dependency, my root issue. I found myself emotionally attaching to a friend named Lindsey. It wasn't as strong of a dependency as I had in the past, but it was still an issue.

"Lord," I prayed one day, "what do you want me to do for full deliverance from emotional dependency?"

God led me to stop contacting Lindsey, and to start making new friends. I was to take the knowledge I had and live out my deliverance by mentoring women in recovery who truly needed my attention.

While I spent my time mentoring, I grieved the loss of the friends I was emotionally dependent on. It took energy and work to be strong for myself and take responsibility for my own emotions. I grieved over my failures in those relationships, but I also moved forward and forgave myself.

When I started relating to others in a healthy way, I realized in the past I had unrealistic expectations of my friends. I wanted them to meet my emotional needs, which was something only God and I could do. The process of deliverance from emotional dependency took months. Little by little, God changed my whole perspective of life and how I related to people. One day, I realized God delivered me. He brought me to a new level, and a new season of life I had never experienced before.

My deliverance from emotional dependency was greater than any other deliverance in my life because it was the root of all of my other addictions and problems. I thank God for His delivering power in my life. I love to testify of this major miracle.

Grace

I was angry when I found out someone I was close to was struggling with addiction. It frustrated me that this person I loved so much refused to seek help to recover from addiction.

My Aunt Sara could not believe my attitude. "Angel, you are angry that this individual chose the wrong path. Do you think that just because they know about your situation and your story, it should have prevented them from going down that path?"

I thought about it for a moment, then said, "Yes, ma'am. That is what I think. Why not learn from my mistakes instead of ruining their life?"

"Angel," Aunt Sara said, "Do you remember what you were like before? You weren't open to what anyone said when they tried to help you recover from active addiction. That's where your friend is at right now. Be patient and understanding. Show her the grace your family and friends showed you."

I realized I had been drug free, sober and saved for so long that I had forgotten what it was like living in bondage to addiction. I was convicted because of my lack of compassion for my friend. I was not set free from addiction just for spiritual wholeness for myself. I was set free so that I could help others find freedom.

Everyone grows and changes at a different pace. It is not my place to set a deadline for deliverance or healing. It is not my place to judge whether another person is sincere or not.

With my change in attitude, I began contemplating the process of deliverance. How can a person repent and begin to find deliverance from sin if they don't even know what sin is? Addicts seeking recovery need a strong voice in their life to mentor them in what to do. Love and compassion should stir people like me to confront addicts with grace. Someone has to step up and bring them a message of hope and help. I decided as long as I had life in my body, I would be that voice to others. I committed to speak the truth in love as Ephesians 4:15 commanded.

Sharing My Testimony

After my process of delivery from emotional dependency, opportunities became available for me to share my story, both in recovery and church settings. I never declined an opportunity. One of the first times I gave my testimony was at a church in New York City. I was there singing at a gospel choir concert when I was asked to share some of my testimony.

I held the microphone and began to share. "God brought me out of addiction, but not only that, He restored my relationship with Him after I had walked away from Him. He saved me! God doesn't care about social class. God doesn't care about how far into sin you have gone. If He was able to draw me out of a lifestyle of addiction, then He can save you out of your situation!

"Acts 10:34-35 says, 'Then Peter opened his mouth, and said, Of a truth I perceive that God is no respecter of persons: But in every nation he that feareth him, and worketh righteousness, is accepted with him.' It doesn't matter who you are, or where you came from, God has a plan for your life. He loves you!"

When I first began to speak, I wasn't comfortable to share that I had once been a prostitute or that I was HIV positive. Overtime, I began to gain confidence and open up more as I testified.

"85 percent of women involved in prostitution are addicted to drugs. At age 19, I became addicted to crack cocaine. I started prostituting just before I turned 20 years old. The biggest lie I told myself was that I could control my addiction, and that I could stop whenever I wanted to. I couldn't control it. I was out of control.

"I lived on the street until September 6, 2002 when I stood in a courtroom and a judge had mercy on me. I was 23 and a half and I have never used drugs since. I surrendered my life to God a few weeks after that court date. Then, at age 24, I was diagnosed with HIV and Hepatitis B. At age 32 God healed me from Hepatitis B! Now, though I live with HIV, my levels are undetectable—I'm the healthiest I can be with HIV."

After one service where I shared my testimony, I walked into the church prayer room and an elderly woman approached me. She had white hair that was tied up in a bun on the top of her head. Her skin was wrinkled from years in the sun. She wore a long dress that draped from her neckline to her ankles.

"Angel," she said with a crack in her voice. "That was a brave thing you did sharing your testimony out in front of everyone like that."

I nodded my head. I couldn't help but wonder what this woman thought of me. I had just announced to the entire congregation that I used to be a prostitute. Would she judge me?

"Angel," she continued. "Don't you let anyone make you feel bad about selling your body for drugs and money." Her words caught me off guard. Is it possible she didn't think badly of me? The woman's face tightened. "After all," she said, "the girls around here are giving it up for free! So the way I look at it is that at least you got something out of it!" I still laugh about her perspective today, and how it caught me off guard.

Something funny happened recently when I was invited to speak at an addiction ministry of a church a few hours away from where I live. I printed directions and brought a person I sponsor in recovery along with me on the trip. I stopped to buy a cup of coffee and called the man at the church who invited me to speak to let him know where we were. "Well great!" He said. "I'll see you in a few minutes."

I thought I still had fifteen minutes to drive. I got back in the car and continued down the road. When we arrived at the church, the parking lot was empty except for a few church vans, so I drove around the church looking for someone.

"These people are so rude. They didn't even send someone to come look for me, and I'm their guest speaker. No one is even here!" I was frustrated and decided to call the man again.

"Hey, where are you?" I asked.

"I'm outside looking for you. Where are you?"

"I'm driving in circles around the church, and I don't see you anywhere."

That's when it occurred to both of us that I was at the wrong church. I was supposed to speak in twenty minutes, and I had driven fifteen minutes too far in the wrong direction. I quickly headed back through town and walked into the room just in time to hear the man introduce me as the speaker!

Whenever I'm speaking, either at church or in a recovery setting, I love to tell about a conversation my mother and I had that helped me take responsibility for my life choices and to quit blaming others for life's unfairness.

I spoke to the crowd as I shared my mom's words of wisdom. "My mom looked me straight in the eyes and said: 'I refuse to allow you to manipulate me with obligation and guilt because I wasn't the mother you thought I should be. You are not going to throw who I was in the past in my face, or use me as an excuse for your problems. I will not feel guilty because of your choices.'

"And what she said was right," I continued. "For so long I used people as an excuse for my poor choices instead of taking responsibility and making the right choices for myself.

"Many people in active addiction point to all of the unfair parts of their life—the abuse, neglect, rape, all of these horrible and painful things they have experienced—to justify why they use drugs. But the truth is, there are a lot of people who have been through the same kinds of horrible events, and they don't use drugs to deal with their problems.

"We all have negative life experiences. I may not have the same problems you have, and you may not have the same problems I have, but we all have the power to make a choice on how we will respond and deal with our lives. It is your choice."

Mentoring and Self-Care

Along with public speaking, I spend time mentoring women in recovery. One day, I was on the phone with Holly telling her about someone I was mentoring. The girl constantly called and texted me if she was in an emotional crisis. I asked Holly how I should handle the situation.

Holly gave me great advice. "If you interrupt your day and neglect your responsibilities to cater to her when she has a crisis, then she is going to expect that every time. Do not stop everything in your life just because she is having an emotional meltdown. Keep your priorities in line. Call her when you get off work and when you are ready to listen to her crisis."

I decided that self-care has to be my priority if I am going to continue mentoring others. I don't put their needs before my own, and I'm not consumed with fixing their problems. Now, when I first begin to sponsor or mentor someone, I make sure they understand it is their responsibility to call me if they need help.

"I'm not chasing you down. You need to call me if you need me," I tell them. "But remember, I also have a life and I work, so I may not be available every time you call me. You need to build a support network of five or six stable people that you can call to help you in your recovery. It is impossible for one person to be everything to you. I'm not Jesus. I'm not your Savior. I cannot rescue you every time you have an emotional crisis."

I'm a voice in their life, but I'm not the only voice in their life. I know I'm mentoring people who have the potential to be better leaders than I am. I want them to take responsibility for themselves from the beginning. I refuse to allow the women I mentor to totally depend on me. That is something my mentor, Theresa, taught me by example long ago.

I also tell them, "If you relapse while I am mentoring you, I'm not going to lose sleep over it. I have nothing to do with your choices. When your pain is bigger than your fear of change, you'll change."

That may sound harsh, but I have learned not to emotionally attach myself to the outcome or response of the people I mentor. Of course, I'm curious and I care about them, but the choices they make don't control me or affect me emotionally.

Mentoring others requires grace, patience and staying optimistic. Here is a list I have made of my priorities as a mentor and sponsor:
- Pray for them everyday
- Listen
- Speak the truth in love
- Encourage them when they make mistakes

- Love them unconditionally no matter what
- Show them a different perspective
- Confront them when they are wrong
- Live as a Christian example for them to follow
- If I make a wrong choice, make amends immediately
- Always admit when I'm wrong

Maintaining My Deliverance and Recovery

I strive to always keep the promise I made to God long ago, that every choice I make in life would be for His glory. I asked God to show me what I can do to bring Him glory. He spoke to my spirit this simple phrase: *I receive glory every time you choose to do the right thing.*

For me, the right thing means I must maintain my deliverance and recovery. I maintain by keeping my boundaries strong, going to recovery meetings, and making good choices one day at a time. I work to keep the door of temptation to addiction shut and the door to healthy relationships open. I strive for balance, consistency and perseverance.

I avoid procrastination. If I mess up, it is my job to make it right as soon as possible. I keep moving forward even when I don't feel like it. I don't live by how I feel, but by what I know.

I am thankful for the grace of God in my life. I'm thankful for everyone that has helped me along the way, and for all the people I've had the opportunity to help. This year, I celebrated 10 years since beginning of my recovery journey. I've learned much, and I have much more to learn. No matter what challenges I face tomorrow, I will remember what my grandma always tells me: "You've come a long way, Baby."

Thank you for allowing me to share my experience of recovery, my relationship with God, and what I know about spiritual freedom and emotional wellness. I shared my heart here and what has helped me to change. I hope many of you will find hope through my story.

I am happy to share what God has done for me. I humbly admit that I still have problems, and I'm still learning about myself. I am not ashamed that I am HIV positive.

I want to share two more verses with you. Revelation 12:11: "And they overcame him by the blood of the Lamb, and by the word of their testimony; and they loved not their lives unto the death." And Jeremiah 29:11: "For I know the thoughts that I think toward you, saith the Lord, thoughts of peace and not of evil, to give you an expected end."

WHO JESUS IS

Jesus is the Parent Who never failed.

Jesus is the Lover that never rejects, abuses or abandons you.

Jesus is the Healer when the doctor says healing is impossible.

Jesus is the One who asks you to dance when no one else did.

Jesus is the Friend when everyone else walks away.

Jesus is the Comforter in times of grief.

Jesus is there when I wake up happy for no reason at all.

Jesus is the One that doesn't need an explanation for why you are hurting. He already understands.

Jesus is the Strength that empowers you when you don't think you can face another day.

Jesus is the One that didn't give up on you when you gave up on yourself.

Jesus is the One who takes up for you when no one else speaks up in your defense.

Jesus is the One who helps you get up after you fall flat on your face in front of the whole world.

Jesus is the supernatural peace you have while facing a fearful and unknown future.

Jesus is the light at the end of the tunnel.

Thank-you Jesus for all you are to me, and for who you are to each of us. I did not deserve the chance to change my life.

Jesus gave me the opportunity to change and for that I will forever give Him the glory He deserves.

Childhood photo,
Angelena Cortello

Angel, age 19, just prior to
crack addiction

Angel, 23 years old, during
active addiction, 89 lbs,
prior to last court date

Angel, 2013, age 33

Bipolar Disorder

Bipolar Disorder is a mood disorder in which people experience episodes of mania alternating with episodes of depression, which interferes with daily life.

Symptoms of manic episodes:
- An increase in energy
- Decreased need for sleep; active for days with little or no sleep
- Racing thoughts
- Overly talkative
- Low attention span
- Easily distracted
- Grandiose thinking
- Feelings of euphoria
- Spending sprees
- Engaging in risky behavior
- Increase in sex drive
- Delusional ideas
- May indulge in substance abuse to relieve symptoms

Symptoms of depressive episodes:
- Suicidal thoughts
- Decrease in sex drive
- Loss of interest in activities usually enjoyed
- Anxiety
- Anger
- Isolation
- Fatigue
- Guilt
- Persistent feelings of sadness, helplessness and hopelessness
- May indulge in substance abuse to relieve symptoms
- Social anxiety
- Lack of motivation
- Loss or gain in appetite
- Sleeping problems

For information on Bipolar Disorder, visit: www.nimh.nih.gov
24/7 National Suicide Prevention Lifeline: 1-800-273-TALK (8255)

Hepatitis B

Hepatitis B is a contagious illness of the liver that may cause cirrhosis and, or liver cancer.

Symptoms:
- Loss of appetite
- Vomiting
- Body aches
- Mild fever
- Dark urine
- Jaundice
- Itchy skin

Hepatitis B can be contracted through:
- Blood
- Childbirth
- Body fluids such as semen and vaginal fluids
- Sharing razors
- Sharing toothbrushes
- Sexual contact
- Transfusions
- Dialysis
- Acupuncture
- Tattooing

Hepatitis B cannot be transferred by:
- Holding hands
- Sharing eating utensils or drinking glasses
- Kissing
- Hugging
- Coughing
- Sneezing
- Breastfeeding

For information on Hepatitis B, visit: cdc.gov

HIV/AIDS

HIV (Human Immunodeficiency Virus) kills t-cells that help the body fight sickness and disease. AIDS (Acquired Immunodeficiency Syndrome) is a disease that develops after HIV has destroyed the body's immune system.

HIV can be transmitted through:
- Unprotected sex
- French kissing with an open sore in the mouth
- Blood, semen, or vaginal secretions
- Sharing needles
- Blood transfusions
- Pregnancy, birth or breastfeeding

HIV is not transmitted through:
- Working with an infected person
- Sweat, spit, or tears
- Sharing clothes
- Drinking fountains, phones, or toilet seats
- Eating a meal together
- Insect bites or stings
- Kissing

For information on HIV/AIDS, visit: cdc.gov

GET TESTED FOR THE VIRUS
For HIV counseling and testing, call the
CDC National AIDS Hotline: 1-800-342-2437

OCD

Obsessive Compulsive Disorder (OCD) is an anxiety disorder where obsessive thoughts produce uneasiness, worry, or fear that can lead to compulsive behaviors. Obsessions are repeated, uncontrollable thoughts. Compulsions are rituals, or behaviors, which are continuously repeated to relieve the anxiety caused by obsessive thinking. Symptoms can be extremely time consuming, causing stress and interfering with daily functioning.

Symptoms of OCD:
- Excessive cleaning or organizing
- Repeated checking
- Excessive hand washing
- Repeated counting
- Skin-picking
- Hoarding
- Relationship related obsessions
- Preoccupation with certain thoughts

For information on OCD, visit: www.nimh.nih.gov

Vocabulary

Abstinence: consciously choosing not to participate in an activity one's physical body craves; may refer to abstinence from sexual activity, food, drugs, etc. (Romans 8:13; Acts 15:20; Colossians 3:5)

Acid: a hallucinogenic, called LSD; does not produce a physical withdrawal; could cause permanent hallucinogens that lead to schizophrenia

Addiction: a compulsive need to use a habit-forming substance; physical or psychological dependence on a behavior or substance

Administrative Probation: in Florida, a form of state-supervision in which an offender deemed to be low-risk to the community is allowed to leave the state and be in non-reporting status while finishing out the terms of the probation

Altar: the place a person comes to God, often kneeling; in a church the altar area is often at the front of the church and is a place where people come to pray, repent, and dedicate their lives to God; comes from the Old Testament practice of offering animal sacrifices on an altar for forgiveness of sin

Anemia: a blood disorder in which a person's red blood cells, or concentration of hemoglobin, is low; may be caused by low iron

Anointing: a religious tradition and symbolic process during prayer of applying a dab of oil to an individual, usually a small dot on the forehead; anointing oil represents the Spirit of God that covers and protects an individual spiritually (Exodus 29:7; Mark 6:13; James 5:14)

Baptism: the Biblical command of immersion in water for remission of sins (Mark 16:16; Acts 2:38; Acts 10:47-48)

Bus Ministry: a service that provides a ride to church for people, often children, which do not have transportation

Clean: drug-free

Crack: a solid rock form of cocaine in which is smoked through a glass pipe, an illegal drug

Crack House: a house where people specifically use and sell crack cocaine

Conversion: changing to a new faith or set of religious beliefs (Acts 3:19)

Conviction: 1. a formal announcement that a criminal suspect is guilty of an offense; 2. in the spiritual sense, a very strong belief or opinion said to come from God or a supernatural revelation

Dealer: a person that sells illegal drugs

Deliverance: to release or set free from sin and spiritual bondage including addiction, unforgiveness, bitterness, sickness, etc. (Matthew 17:18; Mark 5:1-20; Luke 4:18)

Detoxification (Detox): The process of physical and psychological withdrawal while discontinuing use of illegal substances

Faith: belief and trust in God and His Word (Hebrews 11; 11:6)

Fasting: physically abstaining from food, or any other specified activity for a period of time while praying, submitting oneself to God, and resisting temptation (Matthew 6:16-18, Matthew 17:21, Jonah 3:5-10)

Feening and Jonesing: an addict's experience of anxiety, craving, and urge to use crack cocaine

Felony: a crime, more serious than a misdemeanor, which may be punishable by one year in prison or more, up to the death penalty

Fornication: participating in sexual activity outside of marriage, a sin according to the Bible (1 Corinthians 6:18-20, Galatians 5:19-21, Ephesians 5:3)

GED: General Educational Development, test that assesses basic education equivalent to a high school education

Hit: one piece of crack, pot, acid, etc. (for example, "I took a hit of acid")

Holy Ghost/Holy Spirit: the Spirit of God as He interacts with humanity (John 14:26, 1 Corinthians 6:19, 1 Corinthians 2:13)

Intercessory Prayer: praying for someone else's needs, asking God to intervene on behalf of another person or situation, also called interceding (1 Timothy 2:1, Romans 8:26, Ephesians 6:8)

Ministry: occupations of preaching, teaching, praying, or other positions of serving a church congregation; also acts of kindness and selflessness that benefit another person (Acts 6:4, Ephesians 4:11, 2 Timothy 4:5)

Mentoring: the process of teaching through friendship; also called discipleship

Pimp: A man that connects clients and prostitutes, and controls all of the money involved; is in total control of the prostitutes; often uses fear, intimidation and violence to control prostitutes

Prison Ministry: A church service that takes place in a prison with prisoners

Recover: a process of restoration that may be physical, spiritual, emotional, etc.; healing takes time and is not an instant miracle (2 Corinthians 5:17, Luke 4:18)

Recovery (Addiction Recovery): the process of regaining health or wellness which often requires following a program or regime as prescribed by a doctor; in this case, actively pursuing recovery from addiction by participating in a program which includes following lifestyle principals and engaging in small group discussion

Rehabilitation, Rehab: A substance abuse treatment center where addicts and alcoholics go to learn how to recover

Repentance: the act of stopping sinful behavior and beginning behavior pleasing to God; a Biblical mandate for salvation (Acts 2:38, Acts 3:19; 2 Chronicles 7:14)

Restore: the process of returning to a previous state, in this case returning to spiritual purity and innocence through a lifestyle of repentance and recovery (Psalm 51:12, Joel 2:25-26, 2 Chronicles 7:14)

Runner: A person who goes directly to the dealer, picks up drugs and brings them to the addict so that the addict doesn't have to interact with the dealer themselves; usually walks or rides a bike; the runner gets a portion of the purchased drugs called "a break"

Skin Picking: DSM-V classifies Dermatillomania or Excoriation (Compulsive Skin Picking) as a diagnosable disorder often preceded by strong tension or anxiety, and followed by relief or pleasure

Soul: a person's innermost being; according to the Bible, the part of a person that lives forever either in heaven or hell (1 Thessalonians 5:23, Psalm 16:10, Matthew 10:28)

Speaking in Tongues: a physical sign that a person has received the infilling of the Holy Spirit, consists of the person speaking in a language they never learned as the Spirit of God flows through them (Acts 2:1-47, Acts 15:11)

Spiritual: pertaining to the unseen realm of God and the supernatural, angels and demons, eternal life, morality, and divine inspiration and revelation

Spiritually Minded: a person who is aware of God and constantly thinks on the scriptures and spiritual ideas (Romans 8:6-8, Romans 12:2)

Testimony: a person's story of overcoming obstacles, usually through faith, divine intervention, or a series of events (Revelation 12:11, 2 Timothy 1:8-9)

Turning a Trick: the act of prostitution, selling one's body for money

Undetectable: a person with HIV who is undetectable is doing very well; they are as healthy as they can be with the virus, their t-cell count can be the same as people without the virus, the amount of the virus in the viral count is low

Will of God: God's sovereignty, God's way—verses human will and desire (Romans 12:2, Psalm 37:23, Mark 14:38)

Worship: a lifestyle of gratitude and adoration to God and obedience to God's Word (John 4:24, Psalm 95:6, Psalm 34:9, Hebrews 13:15; Titus 2:12-13)

Our Written Lives
book publishing services
www.owlofhope.com

Lightning Source UK Ltd.
Milton Keynes UK
UKHW021157220421
382437UK00009B/1631

9 780989 407007